Notes of Ingress

by

Cain Helsson

Notes of Ingress

Fonts: Eagle Lake & Gingerbread Initials

Author

Cain Helsson

Illustrators

Fares Kaze

LCF

Spirit Mediums

Emmerich Weissager

Colette Luneville

Luca D'Ombra

Cain Helsson

Arthur Veil

Notes of Ingress

With deepest thanks, I do render due acknowledgment unto the worthy contributions of Maria Panzona, Thorkell Guðbjartsson, Jäckel Koller, Andrea Cattaros, Gamba Secura, Lucifer, Paulo Gasparutto, Crot, Διαγόρας ὁ Μήλιος, Donna Florida Basili, Olivo Caldo, Catarina of Bastia, Anna la Rosa, Barbara Kollerin, Asru daughter of Ta-di-amun and Pa-kush, Nicolò Colautto, Þorbjörg lítilvölva, Θεόδωρος ὁ ἄθεος, Bridget Ellen Early, Adna mac Uthidir, Ἀπολλώνιος, Volusius Caesario, Christina Rosadoni, Kiyanna Reynard.

FOREWORD

This book is not a work of fiction, nor of scholarship as convention would know it. Notes of Ingress emerges from the marrow of the living, the dead, and that which lies between. It is a collaboration not of authorship alone, but of possession, vision, and spirit-congress. In its making, Cain Helsson served as scribe and witness, transcribing transmissions voiced through the bodies of fellow initiates–Arthur Veil, Emmerich Weissager, Colette Luneville, and Luca D'Ombra–each one momentarily relinquished to entities beyond the veil. Among them: the dead, the never-born, and a figure naming himself Lucifer, who may once have walked Europe's soil under the name Crispen.

The structure of this volume resists linearity and comfort. At times, three voices overlap within a single passage; spirits contradict, harmonize, or distort one another's messages. The living, too, are not exempt from this multiplicity–layers of ancestral and personal knowledge interweave with inherited ritual, yielding a style deliberately disorienting, yet true to the nature of spirit contact. It is not meant to be read as one might a history book, but rather endured, traversed, and surrendered to–like a rite.

Visual elements have passed through the hands of more than one medium. The initial artist vanished–

circumstance unclear–and was replaced by Kiyanna Reynard, whose work, though potent, diverged from the project's envisioned aesthetic. The task then fell to Fares Kaze, whose illustrations finally crystallized the vision: infernal, classical, and alive. These images are not decorations but transmissions in their own right, conjured under the guidance of Lucifer himself.

Notes of Ingress is not composed for the curious or the casual. It is for those standing within–or just beyond–the circle of initiatory fire. It speaks most clearly to those who have already received. And yet, even for them, this book offers no plain teaching. It is a mirror, a blade, a maze, a key. And like all such tools, it may wound as easily as it opens.

Let those who read proceed with offering in hand and familiar at their side. This is not a book; it is a threshold.

Arthur Veil

PREFACE

nlike many who aided me in this work, I am an atheist in worldview. I am also initiated into a few of the main traditions discussed here. I do not personally agree with all the views expressed within these pages.

Information missing from one chapter about a particular tradition can often be found in chapters about other traditions. The techniques and practices are fully revealed, with one crucial exception: the actual initiatory power cannot be transmitted through words. This requires a living custodian to invoke a spirit or witch fire into themselves and channel its force directly into an initiate's body, or in the case of the Mazzeri, is an act of dream invasion.

The initiatory rites given in Tenebrae Draconis are for initiates of that particular tradition (a tradition that's name is intentionally omitted) only and are simply window dressing without a custodian's given transmission. Initiates in that tradition may notice the chant written does not match the one they were given at initiation; this is because it was created while writing this book, as explained in the chapter itself.

Many of the practices described in the chapters can be practiced without the empowerments of initiations. Even if a practice requires a transmission by a custodian to work at the potency intended, there is no harm in a non-initiate performing the rites.

This book, despite not offering the initiations of the main traditions it discusses, does offer an initiatory transmission and is itself an initiation, one particular to this book and its patron: after reading the work three times from cover to cover, performing the prescribed 18 worded conjuration that begins with the word 'Ormur' and offering mentioned in Ignis each time it is read, capable spirit mediums may call upon the spirit of the conjuration to possess them.

This hidden conjuration is not written in the words of the text but is found elsewhere in the book - the easiest of the puzzles to unlock that the book has to offer. Reading the book followed by possession of this spirit will bestow upon the reader witch powers and an initiatory transmission.

Cain Helsson

A tome most dread, wrought by the Devil's hand, wherein the secrets of the departed lie, penned not for piety nor mortal solace, but for the love of Art alone.

In every shadowed line and cursed page, the infernal muse does weave its dark delight, as if to mock the heavens with its craft, and grant to Death a beauty strange and fell.

Contents

PART 1

IGNIS: THE FIRES

A Brief Herald Declaration

Penned by the living author, in concord with his Infernal Maiesty and within the shadowed council of spirit-possessed mediums, whose very lips utter the will of souls long passed. Every passage, the voices of those yet breathing intertwine with the murmurs of the departed. 'Tis a tapestry woven of lived memories both quick and dead.

Every line is touched by spectral hands, as if the shades themselves did guide the quill, lending to each word the weight and wonder of an unseen world. A work crafted as much by the hands of living initiates as it is by the spirits of the dead.

To fashion such a written work hath been somewhat challenging, for the messages of the dead have at times come forth obscurely worded and have required hammering and rewording a few times, that sentences might read with clarity.

The living illustrators, handpicked by Lucifer himself, did labour in dark accord with unseen forces. Guided by spectral channelling and shadowed whispers, their art was shaped not by mortal skill alone but by the mysterious counsel of hidden powers. Thus, did they craft each image, as though spirits moved their hands, weaving infernal visions that serve both mortal eye and unearthly intent.

This tome is fashioned for the initiates of six living traditions, those who have received the sacred empowerments of initiation or stand on its threshold. No initiate of a single path may read only the chapter devoted to their own tradition; rather, each is bound to explore all chapters, for herein lieth knowledge interwoven across all lines of craft. Yet, even this doth but scratch the surface of its mysteries, for the book itself is no mere work of written words. There lie yet veiled depths, and realms of understanding that none but the earnest seeker may uncover, unfolding layer upon arcane layer.

Venture not into these pages alone, but in the company of the familiar spirit, or with the very spirit whose conjuration lieth secreted within these leaves, which must be recited nine times, holding the book in hand, present one's offering of potent liquor in a glass unto the Devil himself. For these pages are not but ink upon parchment, but vessels to summon that which dwelleth beyond the veil, awaiting the conjurer's command. Let not one's journey be one of solitary contemplation, but be guided by the presence of such otherworldly companions, that one mayst uncover the mysteries therein hidden.

PART II

BARBARUS: THE BARBARIANS

On the Rites of the Barbarians

(Herein is gathered the lore of those peoples whom Rome once named barbarous–their rites, spirits, and mysteries laid bare through fire-lit memory and the breath of the dead.)

When the northern barbarians first learned to inscribe their thoughts in the lofty Latin script, leaving behind their brief runic written spells and charms, they crafted long and wondrous accounts, not only of their gods, but also of their mortal ancestors in tales they called sagas.

In these sagas, one might behold the daily life and beliefs of these folk, a strange mingling of the mundane and the mystical. These many Bible-lengthed manuscripts, do speak of warriors, witches, and peasants alike, who would fall into trances beneath the shadow of their hoods, or lie as though lifeless, while their spirits took flight. In this enchanted state, they would assume the form of beasts–wolves, serpents, fish, eagles, or bears–and travel afar to spy upon their enemies or strike them down from distant lands. They called this hamhleypa, "shape-leaping," and hamfarir, "shape-journeying,". These marvels of metamorphosis, the body resting while the soul did soar, were not counted witchcraft, but natural wonders within the reach of all but the lazy.

Dreams, too, were doorways to the spirit world. The dead often spake to the living in visions of the night. If one sought the counsel of a long-departed kin, they would lay themselves to sleep atop the burial mounds of their ancestors. And lo! The dead would answer. Burial mounds, were often raised upon a family's land, that they might dwell near to the spirits of their forebears. For in their faith, where the bond with the dead is held of greater weight than with the gods themselves, it is the custom to build a cairn of stones for the mothers of the line, and another for the fathers.

DE SACRIFICIIS ET MANIBUS

At the fall of Autumn, the matron of the household would make offering of beer, and pour the blood of beasts upon the stones for the fathers, and upon the eve of Winter, or Christmas-tide, for the mothers, in supplication for health, for healing, for fertility, and for fruitful harvests. 'Tis said that the spirits hold fresh blood of the slain, poured upon the stones, in far greater esteem than gold or silver.

In the customs of the Old World, the craft of offering life's force requireth a perception beyond the five senses, that one may know whether the spirit summoned be truly present, and whether it hath accepted the gift. For when the offering is embraced, the spirit's presence doth wax in strength, signifying its acceptance of the gift bestowed.

Should the matron be absent, then another kinsman doth take upon them the rite. The ceremony beginneth with a salute unto the spirits, placing cups of beer before the stones for them to drink, and then a chant, a mantic verse, is sung or spoken to summon forth the ancestors, with words most true to the lore, to be avoided of any elaboration or personal touch. There be no songs of tradition, save for the ways in which they are composed. The chant is recited until a presence, tangible and intoxicating, doth descend from the outer realms, a palpable force that cometh not from inspiration, but from a plane beyond the world we know. Then the blood of beasts is poured into a bowl, and offered upon the stones.

Once the offering is made, the practitioner entereth a silence, open to receive the subtle or bold impressions sent from the spirits. Should the seer be skilled, a dialogue may ensue, one's faculties attuned to the unseen world.

Be aware, too, of creatures that cross path; black beasts are a sign of favour, while white beasts bode ill. Yet, should dwelling be in a place swarming with gulls or crows, such omens are rendered void, for the abundance of beasts of one hue doth cloud the reading.

These offerings may be made throughout the year, or not at all, yet it is deemed most auspicious to perform them at these appointed times. Many are the customs by which one may commune with the dead, and some even journey unto the land of the departed, to speak face to face with those who have passed beyond the veil.

DE VIA MORTUORUM

The wayfaring map to the realm of the dead is clear and easily followed, unlike those of other cultures. This road they call Helvegr, the way to Hel, a dark and mist-shrouded journey that leadeth to a world mirroring our own, akin to the Egyptian afterlife known as the Field of Reeds within the Duat.

Here I shall give one direction to go to Hell.

First, one must needs be a wayfarer of the soul, one who can forsake the flesh and journey beyond the limits of the body. Second, with eyes closed, through clenched teeth, hiss a galdr of the road to Hel, until a vision of darkness and mist does rise before thee. Or, alternatively, close eyes and sink into the blackness and silence; then, with spirit unloosed, journey forth into the void. Whisper then this charm.

"Who treads the road through mist and night,

where shadows close and stars take flight?

The river roars, the waves do rise,

bring forth the bridge before mine eyes.

Bridge, appear, o'er raging tide,

and let me cross where shadows bide."

Notes of Ingress

Now, follow these instructions on the other side.

Part from the mortal frame, let the soul descend in quest, to the realm of shades. Downward must one go, northward too the path shall lead, into dark and mist. Seek the shadowed bridge, cross the river, fierce with torrents, its roaring depths unchained. Further one shall wend, ever downward, northward still, till a gate appears. Pass not its arch, over the wall the way must climb, to the realm of the dead.

There they dwell as we, in a world like unto ours, yet in death's domain. If at some point in life, one hath read from these pages, the guardian of the bridge, Móðguðr, shall grant passage.

Hel, a realm of diverse souls and shifting lands, where even the gods, when death does lay its hand upon them, must make their journey. Here, all nations and creeds are found 'mongst the dead, no immortal walks the fleeting world of flesh, for in the end, Hel does claim them all.

Hel is a gate through which the otherworldly realms, held within the compass of the mighty Tree, are trod; 'tis the Serpent's path. And in like manner is Óðinn a gate, a spirit by whose art whate'er spirits one wouldst call—be it fair or fell—may be drawn forth and stand before you.

The barbarian's reckoning of life and death is a curious and labyrinthine web, woven with strange and wondrous threads, where obscure beliefs entwine about the soul's mystic bond to the birth of land-wights, its sojourn in otherworldly realms, and its ceaseless voyage through deaths and rebirths. At times the soul does wear a mortal form, and at others a spirit's guise, yet these seeming contradictions are but harmonious facets of one singular journey. To grasp this enigma, one must hearken to the cultic tales of Helgi.

Helgi Hundingsbane, fallen in battle, was borne unto Valhǫll, the hall of the noble slain in the realm of the gods, which we in these latter days liken to joining the wild hunt's ghostly host. Yet even in Valhǫll, his spirit would often steal forth to visit Sváva, his wife who still dwelt among the living. When Sváva's mortal span was ended, both she and Helgi were born anew in fleshly guise, and once more did they find union in marriage upon the earthly plane.

Though I shall forbear to unweave the deeper intricacies of this worldview—for these be but the simpler strands of the web—one should'st lend thine ear to the hallowed tales of Olaf Gudrødsson's soul's journey. In death, he was transformed into Olaf Geirstad-Alf, a spirit bound to the land, and thereafter was born anew as Olaf II Haraldsson, a man restored to mortal guise. Yet within this tale lie subtleties that far surpass the common cycle of man to land-spirit and spirit to man, hinting at mysteries that murmur of truths beyond the grasp of mortal wit.

DE POSSESSIONE ET VATICINIO

The barbarians hold a custom most curious, known as *night-sitting* or *sitting out*, wherein a soul doth seek a place of solitude and profound silence in the dark hours. Sometimes armed with weaponry and encircled by a protective fence, yet often without such guard, the seeker doth call forth the spirit of the dead, or perchance a *troll*—a name given to spirits of malefic bent. In solemn silence, they enter a trance most deep, wherein their soul, made receptive, doth perceive and commune with the summoned shade. This practice seemeth the twin art of scryer and conjurer united, such as found in Solomon's grimoires of *nigromancy*, but here devoid of spirit threats or invocation of god-names. At times, the spirits do appear as insubstantial phantasms, mere shadows of form; yet other times, so vivid is their semblance that the very senses are deceived, and one believeth them to be of flesh and blood, though they be but spirits. This *sitting out* hath power not only to summon spirits but to unveil visions unbound to any conjuration, revealing truths and mysteries unbidden.

There is, likewise, another art of nocturnal craft, an oracular rite named *night-walk*, wherein one doth pace with measured step beneath the moon's pale eye, threading often through untamed wilderness or the solemn precincts of ancient graves. As the wanderer doth proceed, they sink by slow degrees into a waking dream, wherein spirits rise and visions strange unfold. This path requireth no guide save that intuitive spark that stirreth within; to descend into such dreams is a gift of the soul, and whosoever can make that fateful leap doth wield the art. This practice must be wrought in utter silence, within and without; heed not the company of men, nor yield to laughter, nor bow to fear.

Gaze not into the fire, nor seek the light, but let shadow and darkness enfold thee, for there do visions spring forth most freely. Cast thine eye through humble keyholes, and thou shalt espy realms beyond; incline thine ear, and the murmurs of the dead shall breathe their secrets unto thee. Upon the fateful *night-walk*, one may, by the spirits' favour, chance upon a wayfarer's hood or a broad-brimm'd hat, lying in wait along their path. These may be donn'd at will, to pierce the veil of shadow with scrying sight, or else a staff of puissant craft, wherein lie nine gates, through which the denizens of the otherworlds may pass into this realm. To be thus gifted by the spirits is the exalted mark of a *night-walker* accomplish'd, one deem'd prepared to receive the hidden lore of occult mysteries.

The *night-walk* is a conjuration utter'd not in word, but wrought in silence–a summoning of the dead, and of the grim, darkly mercurial trickster-spirit Óðinn himself, who appeareth as a swiftly moving shadow, black as pitch, a broad-brimm'd hat upon his head. From out his mouth must one snatch a stick carv'd with burning runes, to receive the power to use the runes with the potent force of ages past. On snatching or dislodging the stick from the Devil's mouth, it shall vanish in an instant, yet the power shall be one's forever.

All nights permit the omens' walk, yet Midsummer and the Yuletide stand most auspicious for such deeds.

Barbarians are vers'd in manifold practices, as to sit beneath the cold and piercing streams of waterfalls, seeking thereby a measure of spiritual ascent; or, when the warmer months do grace the land, to lie beneath the gentler torrents, yet remain untouched by their wet embrace, enwomb'd within a cocoon of great ox-hide or horse-hide, stripp'd from a beast offer'd in sacrifice to the one-eyed god of wayfarers. There, they lend their ear to the ceaseless drumming of the waters' fall, as if Dame Nature herself did strike her secret, hidden drum. By such rites, the soul is borne to the land of the gods, or gifted visions of profound and mighty purpose.

These hides, sanctified by their use, endure the tread of many a rite, and whether lying, sitting, or standing thereupon, no malefic spirit, nor wicked spell, may draw nigh to do one harm, for their virtue shieldeth against all ill.

Notes of Ingress

They hold it true that the common layman, being neither priest nor magician, nor yet witch, may, in the soft and receptive state of wakeful dreaming—whether seated, standing, or in merry dance—serve as an oracle, summoning within their mortal frame the spirit of a god or a departed soul. Such a spirit, taking possession of their earthly form, doth move their limbs as its own and speaketh through their lips, delivering messages unto the living. These arts admit of varying depths: the deeper the trance, the dimmer the mortal's awareness, yet the mightier the oracle's power.

In the furthest reaches of possession, the vessel knoweth naught of what passeth, for the spirit wholly commandeth their form and voice, this being most fit when an audience waiteth to hearken unto the heavenly or ghostly words. Yet, in solitude, shallower trances are more meet, allowing the possessed to behold and hearken unto the spirit's communion, such states being far more ecstatic, imbued with the sweet intoxications of the spirit's essence—each unique and surpassing the raptures of any mushroom's vision or the revelries of the cup.

Still, the oracle, like all who tread the path of prophecy, can but offer that wisdom which their own sight and nature afford. For the clarity and truth of their utterances rest upon their innate gifts as seers, and thus their words must be received as musings to ponder, rather than as certain communions of the spirits themselves.

Notes of Ingress

Ever shall the seer surpass the common layman as a worthy mouthpiece for the voices of the divine.

A seer is no witch, nor is a witch a seer, though at whiles a seer may likewise be a witch. Many are the sacred fields and ancient crafts within the culture's bounds; though their edges may blur, each master walketh a path distinct. Laymen, for all their dabbling, may cast spells or divine shadows of the unknown, yet this maketh them neither magicians nor seers–no more than he who maketh only benches and tables can call himself carpenter. A man may sing or hiss a *galdr*, and with its mantic verse bring death unto another; yet this maketh him not an initiate nor a true magician of *galdr*. It showeth only that he hath sufficient lore to fashion and to voice the *galdr*.

Seers and witches delight in lofts and heights, their art thriving when they are lifted aloft upon raised platforms or seated in exalted chairs. In rapturous swoons they fall, their mortal senses dimm'd, in sweet delirium they float. Their second sight pierceth the veil of the unseen, their congress with spirits is full intimate, and their skill in scrying is hon'd to sharpest edge. They read the fates of men as plainly as if writ upon a scroll and commune with the spirits of the land as freely as one speaketh to a kinsman. Often a choir in song calleth forth these spirits to parley with the seer.

They bear staffs, no mere rods of support, but as sacred pillars, akin to the heart-post of a temple, serving as gateways for spirits of the otherworld to step through. Yet, at times, this staff is wrought not of wood but of iron– an enchanted distaff borne by the witch, wielding the twin powers of a weapon and a tool of fate. It is a thing of awe, binding worlds together and granting its bearer some measure of dominion over the hidden threads that weave the tapestry of existence.

There is a certain practice among their witches, spoken of in hush'd and curious tones, which doth stir within men desires of the flesh akin to those of women, rendering them effeminate in spirit, though not in form. This art, though deem'd unseemly for men to take up, yet ever findeth its willing practitioners among them. Of this, I shall speak no more, for it toucheth upon a carnal commerce 'twixt mortals and spirits (*trollar*), a matter best left unto silence. A singular initiatory rite it is, wherein a man or woman, venturing alone into the far and silent wood, doth invite the spirits to take them by force; and through that strange congress the spirit bestoweth the power of a witch. Yet others there be who, in gentler seasons and within the quiet of their chamber'd beds, offer themselves with willing flesh to such beings in softer wise, that such practices may awaken forces, dormant in the body, to ascend the spine with a lustful nature, stirring the energy with deepened breath; these energies may also be roused by other means deem'd with less cultural shame. 'Tis but one practice 'mongst many that the witches do employ in their craft, and the tradition of the witch doth not depend upon it.

Much like their Celtic cousins, their craft of enchantment doth lie chiefly in spells woven of mantic poesy, wherein the measure of the poetic meter and the reverent heeding of ancestral mythic lore bear greater weight than the rote remembrance of incantations of yore. Yet, let it not be said that no enchanted songs pass down through the lines of descent, for some such airs are preserved, handed from elder to heir. The Celts, with their visionary craft, do employ a means most potent to embolden mantic spells. By murmurous calls, they summon forth the tangible, intoxicating essence of the desired deity. Yet, if this divine effluence be not felt, the rite must not proceed, for to sacrifice in its absence is but to cast gifts into empty air. When the deity's palpable radiance doth suffuse the air, then doth one offer a four-legged beast, spilling its life-blood into a bowl. If rightly performed, this sanguine oblātiō shall make the tangible intoxication caused by the energy swell manifold, as doth distinguish a true sacrificer from a vain slayer of beasts, whose acts bear no fruit but the emptiness of symbolism.

The flesh of the offering is then hewn asunder, cooked and prepared for the faithful (or the lucky) to eat, who partake of its sanctified substance, receiving blessings through this hallowed feast. The poet, a smith of mantic verse, taketh a morsel of raw, reddened flesh and, chewing upon it, is further enraptured by the deity's intoxicating glow, entering an altered state. (Sacrificial flesh shall sooner entrance the mind, yet Adna doth aver that any red meat one may seize shall duly suffice.) Thence, the poet withdraweth to a darkened chamber, where lieth a solitary bed. Upon a slab of stone near the door, the chewed flesh is laid, for there the spirits are enticed to enter; and over this sanguine token, the poet chanteth the verses or plainly speaketh of the desired knowledge sought or the spell to be wrought.

The poet reclineth upon the bed, and with hands uplifted to their visage, doth poetically or plainly beseech that their eyes be opened unto the vision they seek. Their palms then pressed against their cheeks; they descend into a visionary slumber. Upon awakening, they speak once more over their palms and return them to their face, resuming their mystic journey. For three days and nights this sacred cycle endureth, till at last the poet discerneth whether the sought-for wisdom hath graced their soul.

Adna mac Uthidir doth hold this as the key to all things, that shall raise bridges unto what is lost in days of yore.

DE SPIRITIBUS SILVESTRIBUS

Behold, so crude and unrefined are these barbarous folk, that they do regard the trees as kindred spirits, holding firm belief that from driftwood borne of ash and elm, cast upon the shore by the heaving ocean's breath, their lineal descent doth spring. Never having gazed upon the Holy Writ, they lack the lofty wisdom that from earth's dust and a rib's frail curve did humankind arise, and that the beguilement of a serpent, gifted with speech, did thrust our kind into this bitter world. Yet, deeming themselves of the forest's progeny, they grant the trees a solemn reverence, abiding by hallowed rites before the axe is raised. Thus, in their cutting, a tribute is rendered both to the spirit of the tree itself and to any nūminous presence that might therein abide, granting such unseen dweller the grace to flee unhindered to a new abode. To these barbarians, the trees do speak, their voices heard in whispers of the soul, as might the spectres of the dead or other ēldritch beings who make their nests in leafy bowers. Certain trees, by their nature most peculiar, emit æthērial virtues, strong and apt for works of healing, warding, or drawing forth strange visions and dreamlike trances most profound.

Not only doth the barbarian conceive himself a tree, but so too is reality, and the universe both material and divine, of that selfsame tree. Certain trees there be, whose nature openeth portals to worlds beyond our ken. The steed whereon the god of wayfarers doth ride is no mortal beast but a tree—a tree that is reality's essence entire, wherein every soul of man and woman is that tree, and yet the tree remaineth whole and one in all. From the wombs of mothers springeth the fruit of this wondrous tree, and in its branches lie the myriad worlds, each in its appointed place. At the year's waning hour, this mighty tree meeteth its doom, only to rise anew. In that hour of reckoning, a battle rageth—the ending of all things—wherein the gods and their foes perish alike, yet rise reborn, even as the world-tree itself doth spring afresh. 'Tis the end of the world and the world reborn. Such is the eternal rhythm, the cycle unbroken, that unfoldeth with the winter's chill, from December's midmost days to the dawning light of early January.

The Old Testament of Holy Writ doth paint the earth as a flat and steadfast circle, resting firm upon great pillars, and girt about by a vast and boundless ocean; this ocean, in turn, is compassed by mountains, which serve as the foundation for the sky's vaulted expanse. An archangel doth stand in every quarter of the world, each guarding the cardinal points with celestial might. Above this firmament and beyond the shining stars lieth another mighty ocean, and beyond that watery expanse is the hallowed realm of god, where the winged Cherubim and Seraphim do dwell. Beneath the earth, the shadowy domain of Sheōl holdeth the spirits of the departed, and lower still, in the oceanic depths where the earth's pillars do stand, abideth the dread Chaos-dragon of yore.

Yet in the New Testament is this ancient order transfigured, for Jesus doth displace Sheōl with Gehenna, that fiery abyss of eternal torment, where darkness reigneth, and monsters uncountable–fallen angels and the wretched souls of unrepentant sinners–are condemned to suffer everlastingly for their trespasses. To this dread vision, the Church, in their learned wisdom, hath added Purgatory and Limbo, those abodes of wandering ghosts–too virtuous for Hell's flames, yet too stained for Heaven's glory. Meanwhile, the barbarian, in his benighted ignorance, doth imagine the earth and countless other realms as dwelling within the great boughs of a mighty tree; at its loftiest branches percheth a golden eagle, and at its shadowy roots lurketh a vast and baleful serpent, which feedeth upon the corpses of the dead.

In the madness of the barbarian's mind, he deemeth himself to be the very tree, bearing within his bosom all the worlds that do therein abide; yet, in the selfsame breath, he imagineth himself to dwell within the tree, inhabiting its middle realm as one of its countless denizens.

Of the otherworlds that dwell within the boughs of the World-Tree, most do avow their number to be nine; and in charms of second sight, often employed by the barbarian, there lieth a power most strange. For he, gazing upon a forest in this world, may yet behold that selfsame place as it doth appear in one of those otherworlds, where perchance it is no forest but a meadow fair or a bustling village. Thus are the realms upon the Tree's sundry boughs revealed within the workings of the barbarian's mind, coexisting in one place yet sundered far apart, as if by enchantments wondrous and profound. Moreover, the barbarian doth deem that deeds of the past, wrought in some fateful spot, endure still upon some hidden plane, and may be glimpsed as though they linger yet. To this end, he performeth rites of spirit in those very places, seeking to touch the echo of events now passed, believing them to coexist with the present time and the unshaped days yet to come. Such practices, held in reverence, are well favoured in the cold lands of Island.

Most of the denizens that do inhabit the nine worlds of the mighty tree are they that once lived as mortal men, now counted among the human dead. When the barbarian calleth forth his ancestors, or summoneth a spirit of the departed that abideth within these otherworldly realms of the great tree, he doth bid the spirit to 'awake,' as though these realms were but dreams woven by the slumbering dead. Yet other denizens that inhabit these worlds are a race of shape-shifting giants, of whom even the very gods are reckoned as a tribe. Often are they called giants, though their forms be as mutable as the clouds, now towering in vast majesty, now shrinking to the guise of beasts or mighty serpents. In the cultic tales of the barbarian, it is told that these beings intermarried with humankind, and from their mingled blood sprang forth all the ancestors of mankind.

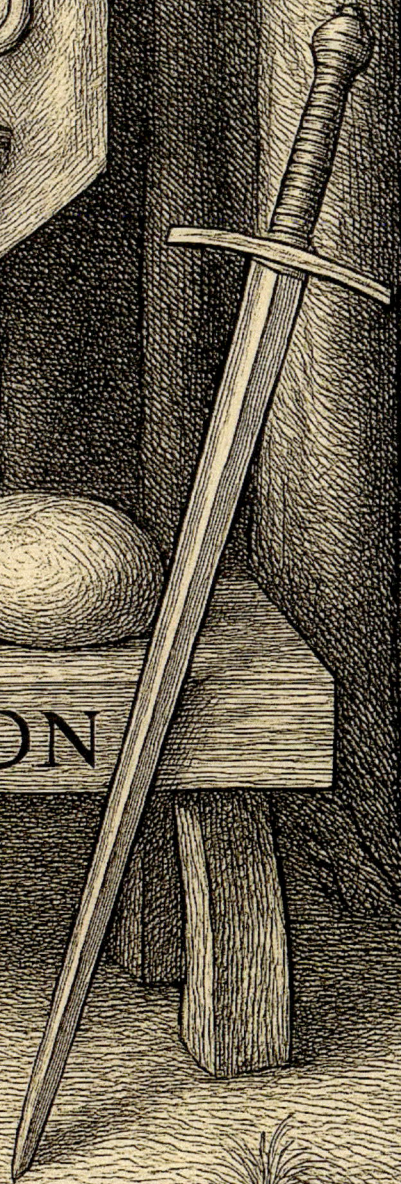

CHAMERON

DE FIGURIS DEORUM ET BESTIIS

To the fantastical beings of the barbarian's lore seem pale and dull when set against the marvels of the Bible. Behold, the *svartálfar, álfar, einherjar, valkyrjar,* and *dísir,* though steeped in mystic charm, appear but as mortal folk sprung from the shades of the departed. Yet, in the sacred tome, angels are no mere men, but fiery flying serpents, wingèd beasts with many heads, and creatures adorned with a thousand eyes and wings, terrible to behold.

Christendom's myriad monstrous forms, where devils and demons, in shapes most dire, do lurk and haunt every shadow. The dragons of the heathen are naught but great serpents; the Bible's, by contrast, are leviathans that Yahweh fights with his thunderous war-club, are of immense girth, stretching for miles, their scales aglow like burnishèd shields, their eyes glow red, their throats spewing fire, and their nostrils belching lightning. Leviathans do bear upon their seven heads full many a horn, as dreadful crowns of might. Dwarves and giants both the heathen tales and Scripture share, yet the Bible doth teem with far more wondrous and otherworldly beings.

Unlike the Bible, the heathen's tales of dwarves and giants are not of flesh and bone, but mere spirits, ethereal and unbodied, wandering the realms of shadow. Likewise, doth the Holy Bible tell of creatures most wondrous and of fleshly form, beings neither mere spirits nor symbolic in nature. The mighty *ziz*, a bird of such vast wingspan as to eclipse the sun itself; its broken egg once loosed a deluge that drowned threescore cities.

Lo, the sea monsters, fire-breathing devourers of whales, seven-headèd leviathans and *tanninim*, and the monstrous *behemoth* of the land, a beast so titanic it doth tower miles aloft. And what of the dragon, whom the prophet Daniel didst smite, or the *tahash*, a one-hornèd wonder with a hide that doth shimmer with all the hues of the rainbow—a creature mistranslated by King James's scribes as the unicorn? In the *Talmud*, too, is told of the *phoenix*, that singular bird who alone among all beasts refused the fruit forbidden from the Tree of Knowledge of Good and Evil.

A noble host of the Church's canonisèd Saints were renowned as valiant slayers of fire-breathing dragons, those monstrous beasts of mortal flesh, whose dread fury slew hundreds of souls each day. Amongst these champions of renown stand St. Theodore of Amasea, St. Romanus, Bishop of Rouen, St. Theodore Stratelates, St. Sylvester the Pope, St. Symeon the Stylite, St. Theodore Tiron, and the illustrious St. George. Yet count I not among these noble dragon-slayers the great St. Michael the Archangel, for he is a spirit, and the dragon he doth vanquish is likewise of a spiritual essence.

Christendom's heavens are a celestial splendour beyond imagining, its hells an abyss of unutterable dread and wonder. The barbarian's otherworld, methinks, is but a drab shadow when held against the vivid tapestry of the Christian vision. If aught, it is Christendom's fashioning of heathen spirits into the creatures of folklore, such as faeries, elves, leprechauns, hobgoblins, and the like, that hath bestowed upon them a hue of allure and a countenance of more vibrant delight.

In the elder beliefs, the variety of spirits is few; and when a spirit is met, twelve feet tall or more, making heavy footsteps upon the earth in the mountains or shadowed forests, it is known as a *troll.* But should it rise to towering height, immense and vast, then it is a *giant.* A spirit that doth shine with a soft or strange light is named *álfar,* yet should it be as a shadow of darkness, it is *svartálfar* or *dvergar,* especially if its form be small and low.

These spirits, all of them, are born of the dead, and they are land-spirits, haunting the wilds and wastes. Some of the dead, having so long dwelt in the wilds, have lost all trace of their mortal shape, but are become strange and other creatures. A warlike spirit, met amid the spectral winds of the Wild Hunt, is called *einherjar* if it be a man, or *valkyrjar* if it be a woman.

26

The dead who haunt the waters, drowning the unwary, may be summoned by music's power to possess the bodies of dancers, and these are called *nix* and *nixe* by the Germans. These spirits may appear as great serpents, monstrous and strange, or as mermen and mermaids, dwelling in the fresh waters of rivers and lakes. And verily, their kin do haunt the salt waters of the ocean, and may be seen upon the waves by those who dwell upon remote shores.

All these spirits of the wild are dangerous to mortal folk, yet may be employed in the arts of magic. With the coming of the Christian faith, these spirits did take on more colourful, strange, and otherworldly forms, appearing as wondrous sights born of the imagination. The few dead and land-spirits that choose to haunt the dwellings of men did become house-spirits, appeased with milk and porridge, to guard the hearth.

In fair Sicilia, the same doth unfold, where pagan spirits of the dead, in the time of Christian rule, are transformed into creatures of a more fanciful and intricate nature, faeries, as it were. Among them, the *Doñas de Fuera* appear, small in stature, men and women garbèd in white, red, or black, their feet the paws of cats. They do play upon musical instruments, dance with mirth, and if anything of Christianity be utterèd in their midst, their anger doth rise like a tempest. They are pleasant to behold whilst they frolic, yet when their jesting ends and their mirth subsides, they take on forms most dreadful–called *ayodons*–and in these shapes, they can bring forth death, slaying mortal men.

Much doth the Basque *Akerbeltz* owe unto Christianity; before the zeal of Christ's disciples swept over the land, *Akerbeltz* was but a humble god, shepherd to flocks and guardian of kine, content in pastoral simplicity. Yet it was Giotto di Bondone, Italy's peerless luminary of the painter's art, who, in a moment of divine inspiration, first did limn the Christian devil adornèd with horns in the thirteenth century. Before his bold stroke, only Moses, Yahweh of the Hebrews of ancient iron-hearted days, and Jesus, as shown in the *Revelation*'s dread vision, were crownèd with such strange adornments in Abrahamic art. This bold imagining did set the course for other hands, who painted the fiend as a minotaur or satyr, and the players of Europe's mystery plays did follow apace.

Thus, was *Akerbeltz*, erstwhile gentle guardian of beasts, raised to the stature of the Devil himself, wielding command over witches and sprites. Likewise, Pan, no longer the merry son of Hermes with pipes and rustic mirth in Arcadia's glades, became the chief visage of Hell's prince. *Azazel*, too, the spirit to whom in the Scriptures goats were sacrificed alongside Yahweh's altar, was by strange alchemy of thought entangled with these goats, until his image grew hornèd and fell. In truth, the hornèd gods owe their renown to Christendom; doubt not they keep a votive lamp ever burning before the name of Giotto.

Amongst the hornèd gods of pagan times, none is more famed than Dionysus, who, at whiles, bore the likeness of a hornèd deity, much as the Minotaurian Yahweh of the ancient Hebrews. His name, *Taurokeros*, proclaimeth him bull-hornèd, and *Tauroprosopos* declareth him bull-faced. Like unto El, the god of Abraham, Dionysus is Lord of the vine, the draught intoxicating, and states of alterèd being; yet the god of Abraham is clad in a far more solemn guise.

In Rome, this Greek god, brought from foreign shores, is hailèd as Bacchus and is often portrayèd, though not invariably, with dainty goat horns rather than those of the bull. A curious kinship he doth share with Óðinn, for both are gods of possession, of frenzies divine, and of manifold ecstasies that pierce the bounds of consciousness. Both are joinèd by the sacred wine; yea, Óðinn is said to live by wine alone. Yet, unlike the revelrous Dionysus, Óðinn doth enjoin temperance in the *Hávamál*, wherefore his wine-fed life is but a poetic veil for hidden wisdoms. Dionysus, contrariwise, is Lord of mirthful revels, the god of feast, of frolic, and of laughter unrestrained.

The barbarian seeketh not to the Bible for counsel in the art of living, but turneth rather to the cultic lays of bards, who sing of heroes and gods with mirthful jests and tales for the delight of children, oft the chief audience of such merriments. Among these, the wayfaring god stands forth—a figure dark and Mercurial, weaving the craft of priests and magicians, as though his deeds were writ in some arcane manual for sorcery. Lo, in some tales, he slayeth himself upon a tree, an offering of himself to himself, much akin to how the Christ, being one with god the Father, suffered death to atone for mankind's trespasses against his decrees. Yet, unlike the Christ, the wayfaring god yieldeth his life in quest of knowledge and wisdom.

Behold, he rendereth also one eye to the depths of a well, that he might behold all things. Yet for all this, never did his followers cast themselves upon trees nor blind themselves of an eye; such self-slaughter or maiming was not their way. Instead, they walked in the shadow of his other deeds, emulating much of what was sung of him in these bardic lays. The barbarian's mind is not bound by simplicity in the reading of these sacred stories; they discern some truths as literal, others as veiled in symbol, and yet others as mere sport for the fancy.

As the Catholic doth kneel in prayer before the mummified, severed head of Saint Catharina of Siena, or the preserved head of Saint Oliverius Plunkett, seeking divine counsel from these sacred relics, so likewise doth the god of wayfarers, the barbarian, hearken unto the wisdom of oracular severed heads. Such is a custom most European, found among many of our diverse kindreds.

Likewise, to parley with skulls is no stranger to barbarian custom, even as Saint Macarius the Abbot did converse with a pagan soul consigned to hell by speech with its barren skull. And lo, the Catholic faithful, in their devotions to the Souls of Purgatory, do adopt skulls from ancient catacombs, granting prayers in exchange for spectral boons, wherein the spirits haunting within grant knowledge or favours material in return for the solace of their intercession.

The spirits of the land, those haunting spectres of the untamed wilds and stewards of each sacred place. In those cultures where men maintain the kindliest bonds with these ancient beings, their cities are of lesser glory, for such spirits do abhor the works of man—those towering edifices that steal from forests their splendour and mar the natural beauty of hill and vale. These spirits, in their bounty, bestow sweet waters from bubbling springs and rich, fecund earth to nourish the farmer's toil. Yet be they perilous to humankind, and oftentimes fierce strife doth arise betwixt these primal powers and those who would push their society toward progress. The barbarian, wise in his simplicity, laboureth to preserve these fruitful alliances and, with cunning craft, doth sometimes seek to sunder his foe's communion with these potent entities.

The barbarians' notions of worship differ greatly from those of Christendom, for their gods did not stand as overseers of moral conduct—such judgments were left to the hands of men and their kin. Nay, their approach to the divine was more akin to barter in the marketplace, where they would proffer sacrifices and offerings in exchange for the boons of favour, and this they called worship. Prostrating before statues and poetic salutes were only polite niceties before initiating this more opportunist behaviour. If the gifts of one god did not suit, they sought out another, as easily as one might seek a better trade. Hence, it was that Norway did once stray from the cross after a hundred winters of Christianity, returning to its old gods, and only by the force of arms was it turned back to the new faith.

Unlike in the faiths of Islam and Christendom, wherein prayers rise to the heavens in one-sided petition, the northern folk do converse with their gods, not as mere supplicants, but as companions in discourse. The common layman, gifted with a medium's touch or skilled in the casting of lots, doth claim dialogue with divinity, receiving answers through the voice of auguries. Yet, though any might engage in such sacred exchanges, the priests and priestesses were accounted more adept in this art, as messengers chosen to relay the will of the gods with greater certainty than the simple souls of the folk.

Their rites were lively, with song and dance, as they marched in procession, their heads anointed with the blood of sacrifice, given unto their gods. Contact with this blood doth stir the mind to ecstasy, more potent even than the strongest of wines, though no drug was mingled in the crimson tide.

Such was the power of this sacred blood that even a man who did not partake in the ritual, but merely stood by and was touched by drops upon his skin, would be seized by a strange, intoxicating fervour and dizzying spell.

If one unacquainted and unfortified in spirit doth come into the influence of such potent energies as are released in the course of these rites, they may find, in the days that follow, that their passions—be they of ire or of desire—are more unruly and harder to tame. Forsooth, these impulses, by nature subdued and ruled by the mind, are magnified by the strange forces unleashed, becoming near ungovernable.

It is a curious consequence of this spiritual intoxication, for while the soul basketh in the warmth and bliss of such contact, it setteth the blood afire and quickeneth the flesh, lifting the body's heat and stirring the lower nature, even as it seemeth, at the moment, sweet as nectar to the senses.

The flesh consumed from the sacrificial beasts—and in some instances, men—whose blood hath been offered unto diverse deities or ancestral spirits, doth fill the body with a most curious warmth and vigour, as if endued with a power that healeth unseen wounds and maketh the labours of life seem but a distant toil. 'Tis said that the very essence of the spirits to whom the blood hath been poured in libation doth pass into the eater, granting a portion of their strength.

The art of sacrifice among the barbarians is a craft most intricate, for it beginneth with a modest offering, accompanied by the recitation of three to nine songs or poems of mantic verse, calling upon the chosen deity to draw nigh. The presence of the divine must be strongly perceived before the sacrificer, be he layman or priest, doth proceed to the second offering, the nature of which is determined by the bargains struck with the god in the course of their communion. This sacred exchange may occur repeatedly, as the number of deities summoned that night doth demand.

DE CANTIBUS MAGICIS

Songs and chants may be performed in diverse manners; yet, in the art of necromancy, 'tis deemed most fitting for words to be hissed through clenched teeth. In contrast, when conjuring magic or stirring spirits to sway the world, a deep humming from the depths of the throat proveth most potent.

The songs and chants that summon the spirits must needs be most exact in their invocation, calling forth the unseen powers with a directness that leaveth no room for vagueness. The verses must be composed in the sacred meter known as *Galdralag*, a rhythm wrought for the weaving of potent spells, conjurations, rites, and ceremonies, wherein *kennings* may be employed to enrich the language. Yet, let no word stray beyond the ancient lore; for to adorn such hymns with elaborate fancies or assumptions not grounded in the time-honour'd traditions is to diminish their power, rendering the works ineffectual to summon forth the spirits sought.

Galdralag, a cousin it is to *Ljóðaháttr*, the "meter of chants," their likeness nigh a mirror. Six lines doth *Ljóðaháttr* hold: the first and second in alliterative bond entwined, the third a solitary voice; then cometh the fourth and fifth, again in paired accord, before the sixth, like the third, doth stand alone. Yet here doth *Galdralag*

35

part its course, for it weaveth unpaired lines betwixt the frame—be they one, or two, or even three. These lines, unbound, do lend their weight to deepen meaning or to echo loud the sixth.

In *Hávamál*'s hallow'd verse are writ eighteen spells most wondrous, known to the god of wayfarers, the wise and wandering lord. Each spell's description, in *Galdralag*'s enchanted measure fram'd, is not mere telling, but the spell itself, the very charm made word. Thus, the speech and the sorcery are one, each utterance a weaving of might and mystery, bound in the cadence of ancient craft.

Presume not to shape the spirits to one's own ideals, but let them manifest as they are, in their true and untamed nature, whether it be pleasing or displeasing to one's own sensibilities. Approach them with a curiosity unfeign'd, a wonder at meeting the unknown, be it fair or foul, gentle or terrible. If spirits of ancient times reveal themselves in monstrous forms, then greet them with the respect due to such powers, for they are mighty and not to be scorn'd. Nor should one take a deity's fiery temper or fierce bearing as a sign of displeasure, but rather acknowledge that they are born of harsher ages, where strength and rage are virtues that drive deeds to swift completion. The gods and shades of the departed may at times don a visage of sweetness and gentle grace; yet, when they unveil a countenance of horror and nightmarish dread, it serveth to awaken the spirit, imparting a vivid sense of existence and the reality of the experience. In such moments, the results that follow are swift and potent, stirring the heart and soul to depths uncharted.

It is of utmost significance to receive an ancestral name, confer'd upon one by either a living custodian of a family's lineage or a spirit of the dead from a lineage of one's blood or other, as was Helgi, who was named by a guardian from the realm of the dead.

Such a naming bindeth one unto an ancestral shade, a spirit who shall abide with one throughout life's course. In many guises shall they appear, whether as beast, man, or otherworldly wight; *álfr, ogre,* or *valkyrja,* all born from the spirits of the dead. Without such a bestow'd name, even if of the same blood, one cannot claim the ancestral dead as guardians.

Nevertheless, those who are without such a name may yet call upon the gods, provided they observe the customs and rites with utmost reverence, as here prescrib'd. For even the unnamed, if they uphold the sacred ways, may find favour and communion with the divine.

When summoning the dead, one must commence with the phrase *'Awake!'* or *'Wake up!'* to rouse them from the otherworldly dreams they may dwell within, whether they inhabit realms of bliss or despair. The dreams of the departed unfold like vast worlds to those who are free from the fleshly bounds of the body.

Avoid the making of oaths at all costs, for oaths are binding chains. One may weave many a falsehood with careless tongue, and such spoken untruths bear no weight, for even the gods themselves are known to play the trickster. Yet, the law of the oath holdeth great import among both the living and the dead, as well as among the divine. Take heed, however, that oaths sworn to those who break their oath bear no significance, nor do forced oaths. Agreements of words hold not the weight of oaths unless one expressly declares, *"I give my oath."*

Be ever vigilant in the choice of one's words when forming pacts and contracts with the gods and the departed. In this realm, where the air is thick with legalities, the spirits may possess minds colder than ice, even those who, in the moment of an accord, may cloak themselves in gentle sweetness.

Words inscrib'd in blood, whether drawn from a vein or mingled with dyes of crimson hue, shine forth to spirits as if penn'd with the fiery glow of night's embers, beckoning them to action, akin to the stirring songs of mantic verse.

When crafting such missives, one must accompany the act with chants of mantic rhythm, either invoking the spirits desir'd or commanding the intent of the written words. Oft are the written words wrought with praise or laced with insult, summon'd forth by the spirits to manifest in the realm of the living.

Praises, like sweet ambrosia, bestow blessings upon those they touch, while insults, dark as a tempest, breathe life into curses that haunt the unwary.

At whiles, written letters do serve as anchors, binding this mortal world to the unseen visionary workings of the spirit that penn'd them, or to the motions set adrift by mantic verses utter'd at their birth.

In such writs, number'd repetitions of letters and hidden codes were known to certain spirits, most notably to the dead initiated in mystic arts. This craft doth unfold a complexity far exceeding the simple scripts engraven on leaden tablets by Greeks, who call'd upon dread *Hecaté* and the departed to fulfil their petitions. Nay, even the Egyptians did pen their missives to the dead, instructing them in the afterlife or moving them to enact desired deeds for the sake of the living.

Verily, as the Christian doth, so too doth the barbarian makes use of talismans, amulets, amber, amethyst, medals bearing the likeness of holy figures, crystal ball pendants for scrying, and other such charms wrought of diverse materials. Yet, perchance, one might say that the Christians possess a greater variety of these sacred things, lacking certain powers and faculties more common among the heathen folk. Amongst the barbarian, there are charms most strange, such as dried serpents, coiled and kept within lockets, fossils, jet, quartz pebbles, spiral serpents, figurines of frogs and serpents, and stones of a serpentine nature–whose meanings, alas, are lost unto us, hidden in the shadow'd past.

Lo, there be charms most quaint and spells of laymen's craft, wherein no art nor skill are required save only faith in the virtues of the *materia*. Behold, the custom of laying seven divers flowers beneath one's pillow on Midsummer's Eve, in hope of dreaming of that future husband or wife whose visage fate hath ordain'd. Or, more darkly, the practice of mingling a madman's powdered corpse within the food of another, with the grim belief that by repetition of this deed, the poor wretch shall be driven to incurable and direful madness. 'Tis believ'd that serpents' tongues possess a talismanic virtue, lending aid to cure madness and maladies wrought by spirits.

To gaze through hag-stones 'twas believ'd one might espy the otherworlds, beholding all things in their most true and perfect essence. Some dare even to wear the skin of a dead man's face, believing thereby to pass unseen amidst their enemies, as if death's own shadow cloak'd their step.

Many such charms do lean upon necromantic art, as in the carrying of a dead man's knucklebones to ward against loss in brawls, yet only with the blessing of the spirit departed, lest the charm turn sour. And yet, not all these fancies hold true substance, for among them are those rumour'd charms that dwell but in the realm of folly. Consider the tale of the pouch of flowering fern seeds, said to grant the wearer invisibility; yet here is a lie most plain, for ferns, in truth, bear no seeds at all. Thus do these curious beliefs flutter like moths 'twixt the candle of hope and the shadow of delusion.

DE MYSTERIIS VETERUM

Such is the spiritual poverty of the heathen barbarian, whose oracles do consult sever'd human heads and skulls, whose groves and temples are made ghastly with the stain of blood, and whose gods delight in strife and death. Their vision of heaven, if heaven it may be call'd, is but a reflection of their own desires, where the soul doth wander blissful, as though basking in the wealth of the earth, but upon fair landscapes of the spiritual realm. Some, more wretched still, do add to this dream a realm where endless battle doth rage–where none die for ever, but after slaughter rise again to feast and drink in great halls, only to engage anew in strife the next day. Alas, there is no ascent to the mystical heights of the wise Agrippa's philosophy here–no vision of eternal joy nor oneness with the very truth of being, no pure communion with the source of all that is, where bliss is the knowledge of all, and felicity a perpetual state. These barbarians remain grounded in fleshly delights, far from the loftier realms of transcendental union with the divine.

No doubt, the fervent rites and ecstatic ceremonies of the barbarians' seasonal festivals do unshackle the spirit from the weight of flesh, and thus make such wayfaring through realms more common 'mongst the folk. The soul, untether'd by these divine frenzies, doth more easily slip its mortal bonds, wandering in vision and trance to far-off places, as if the very winds of the gods themselves do bear it hence. This loosening of the spirit, a gift of their rites, doth transform their world into a place where travel between the seen and unseen becometh as natural as breathing.

Yet, no whisper from the shadow'd days of the pre-Christian Germanic barbarians speaketh of caul-births as making one more skilful in such ethereal arts of wayfaring in spirit.

'Tis only in the later Christian folk customs of those very lands, where the caul doth find its strange relation to such practices. For instance, the curious rite in Scandinavia, wherein a pregnant woman might crawl beneath a foal's caul, stretch'd 'pon sticks, in the hope of easing her labour-pains. Yet, such a comfort came at a cost: her offspring would become shape-shifters and vampire nighthags, doom'd to a devilish fate of heathen practice.

It was also believ'd that to be born with a caul was to be touch'd by powers unseen, bestowing upon the fortunate child the gift of clairvoyance, the power to commune with the dead, and a shield of sorts, better guarding them from the wicked snares of witchcraft. Thus did such beliefs weave their way into the customs of Christian lands, though their origins seem to root in the pagan soil from whence they sprang.

PART III

CLARISSIMO: THE CLARISSIMO CYCLE

On the Hidden Art and Ancestral Fire of the Benandanti

(Herein are gathered the fragments and recollections, the testimonies of the folk, the sayings of the wise, and the visions of the soul unbound—concerning that secret fellowship called the Benandanti, whose paths are marked by caul and calling, whose rites are writ not in ink alone but in the fire passed down through blood and breath.)

In the year fourteen hundred and twelve, Demonologers did pen their accounts of a custom in Germany, which by then had endured the span of centuries, known to the common folk as *Die Ferne Leute*, or *The Distant People*. These souls, blessed—or cursed—from birth by the veil of a caul, were called to bear a sacred duty, set apart from other women and men, to ward off the malefic designs of witches.

Yet mark well, by witches I speak not of those who invoke virtuous and pure Diana, protectress of virgin

44

maids, nor those who cry unto the blessed *Maria* in their rites of healing, and in crafting charms to ward the household. No, the witches to whom these *Distant People* are sworn foes are the *Hexen*, the thralls of diabolical spirits like *Wōden* and the Devil, whose black arts allow them to slip the bonds of flesh and walk in spectral guise as beasts, wolves, and fouler creatures yet.

These, who in their hunger for life prolonged, forsake their human shell to crawl unseen into the bellies of women and beasts, stealing the breath from babes yet unborn, leaving the womb a cradle of death. These, who by night traverse the winds to sever the ghost of a man's phallus, housing it in an elm tree, leaving the poor wretch lusting impotently, or else bound only to the foul enchantress herself. Their deeds are foul beyond measure: in spirit they feast upon the hearts of men, drink of their livers' blood. These witches harbour within their bones a cold and unholy fire, black as midnight, that distorts the very sight of man, casting fearful visions before their waking eyes.

Such were the beings the *Ferne Leute* swore to defend against, battling sorghum with chervil and fennel, darkness with light in a land fraught with nightmarish lore.

DE FERNE LEUTE ET HOSTIBUS MALEFICIS

ennel stalks and other plant weapons, like unto the wands and staffs found in Solomonic grimoires, do serve to sting and vex the spirits and foes, being wielded to bring harm but not death. Such green implements may charm, wound, or chastise, yet the bane of life itself must needs be wrought by iron's cold embrace. When death is sought as an answer to quarrels, 'tis no frail wand that will suffice, but rather an iron distaff or rod that beareth the potency to seal the doom of one's adversary, its touch ushering them unto the dark abysm.

"*Et quidem si puer nascitur in pellicula, dicunt ipsum esse de illis, qui magna spacia in una nocte per transeunt, vulgariter 'die farn leude' etc. Denique homines in hanc labuntur demenciam, ut cultum soli deo debitum ipsis, qui vere demones sunt, exhibeant quosque largitores bonorum false existimant. Sic eciam quidam faciunt in quintis feriis Quatuor temporum et in nocte precedenti quarte ferie Cinerum.*"

– *John of Frankfurt*, in Joseph Hansen ed., *Quellen*, p. 76

The custom of the Ferne Leute, in time, did spread unto southern climes, found new life in Venice, Friuli, and other parts of Northern Italy, where these folk are known by the name **Benandanti**, meaning 'Good Walkers.' And well doth this name accord with their purpose, for these folk journey forth, not in the flesh but in spirit, to contend with witches and evil spirits that prey upon mortal men. 'Tis no wonder such a practice doth flourish in these southern lands, for the forefathers of Northern Italy were once wanderers hailing from Germania, who in ancient days did migrate from those northern realms. Thus, much in their ways of life, their rites, and customs do mirror those of their forebears in regions far as Denmark and beyond. So in this practice of wayfaring, we see but a reflection of the old ways carried far afield by time and tide.

Rosaries and novenas yield far greater fruit than simple prayers, and fasting bringeth results stronger still, yet none of these mayst guarantee success. Likewise, the works of the Benandanti surpass even fasting and prayer, though naught is ever certain. Yet, 'tis known, the labours of the Benandanti are the surest bulwark against the cursed arts of witchcraft. The Benandanti need not be of the Catholic fold; yet, in those days spanning the 4th to 16th centuries, there were Christians–first bred of Catholic, Gnostic, and Arian roots–whose faith's compass was set to the sole purpose of securing a fairer afterlife than the life they lived, while striving to shun a fate more grievous. Such a path left them ill-armed against the potent spiritual arms wielded by the elder European ways. Thus arose the need for orders like the Benandanti. As

Florida Basili did utter before the Inquisitor Father, "Were we not Benandanti, the witches would devour the children, yea, even in their cradles." It taketh a witch to know the dangers of witchcraft.

Who can be Benandanti, what we look for.

Was the soul brought into this world with a caul upon its brow?

Hath the individual beheld any certain premonitions of what yet is to come, in the slumbers of sleep or waking visions?

Whilst lying abed with eyelids shut, hath the individual found their soul and sight to wander beyond the confines of the flesh?

To be born with a caul is held in great fortune, a most auspicious sign indeed. Should a child of Lombard lineage be so graced at birth, such an event doth bind them in duty to become one of the Benandanti. Yet not all Benandanti spring forth with a caul, for this wonder most often accompanieth those birthed prematurely. It is of use to preserve the caul; one must press a piece of parchment upon the infant's visage, whereupon the caul shall cling, thus fashioned into a keepsake. Once dried upon the parchment, it may be sealed within an amulet, to guard its bearer against the blows of witches and elves alike.

In the 1700s did Paolo Molinaris gain his initiation as a Benandante, for at birth he came not merely clad in a caul but with a mouth all ready full of teeth and a large eye, all reckoned as signs of import. To be born mishappen, with locks of hair or some peculiar trait, might mark one's fate as Benandanti; yet far more oft such marks were viewed as brands to seal a witch's fate.

DE CAULIS NATIS ET SIGNIS ELECTIONIS

The steadfast and devoted practice of scrying in the occult arts may bring upon the practitioner certain unintended effects, such as glimpses of that which is yet to come, and visions that linger upon the threshold of sleep, known as *somnia prophetica*. These occurrences, wrought by the mind's deep communion with the unseen, are but the natural consequence of one's persistent gaze into the veiled mysteries.

The chosen must possess a strong inner eye, such that with closed eyes they can conjure the outer world in vivid likeness within their internal vision.

For ninety-nine days, every night, they must lie supine upon their bed, before sleep doth claim them, and again before they rise in the morning, to summon the likeness of their chamber wherein they rest, exploring its every corner with their inward eye; and the longer they linger therein, the stronger their sight shall grow. Let the body lie as one bereft of breath; if it should stir, let it be by its own will alone. Should the flesh itch or yearn for relief, one shalt not attend it, for one art as one dead unto the body's call. Restrain all heed, as though the frame were but a lifeless husk, unmoved and unresponsive to the whims of mortal sensation. When in prayer, the chosen must rise ever skyward, or descend ever downward beneath the earth, soaring or delving in the landscape of the visionary mind.

The deeper within they descend, the farther they roam beyond their fleshly bounds. To ascend unto the loftiest heights of heaven's ecstasy, one must first descend to hell's profoundest depths to find heaven's gate. Even so, the spirit's passage to forsake the body and traverse the realm beyond the flesh lieth in venturing yet deeper within, to find therein the world without. Thus, the way up is down, and the way out is in.

"Ad ambulandum sicut spiritus, primum fac te dominum cubiculi tui. Permitte lapides eius in te vivere, donec caro tua sit velut vestis abiecta." - The Mundusin

DE EXERCITIIS INTERIORIBUS ET VIAGIO SPIRITUS

To the common folk, sleep paralysis is a most curious and eerie affliction, wherein the sufferer, caught betwixt the realms of wakefulness and slumber, finds their body as though bound in chains, wholly immovable. The mind, still conscious, doth stir, yet the limbs remain unyielding, as if frozen by some unseen force. Often in this moment, the senses become as traitorous conjurors, birthing visions and phantoms from the depths of fear - spectres, devils, or dark creatures, all hallucinatory wraiths, visiting the mind like unwelcome guests in this unsettling half-waking dream. The paralysis binds the body fast, yet the eyes may roam and the heart quicken, as the sufferer lies at the mercy of both imagination and this unnatural stillness. In the philosophy of the Benandanti, sleep paralysis is not a cause for dread, but rather a fortuitous threshold, a portal to realms beyond the waking world. Blessed indeed is the soul to whom this moment doth come. In such a state, one must calm the trembling heart and focus the mind, summoning the likeness of their chamber with the inward eye, gazing upon each shadowed corner and hidden nook. Through this envisioning, one may rise from the body and wander forth, much like the Benandanti themselves, or take the shape of a creature, merely by the force of intent. Any spectres or dark phantoms that may appear are not to be feared, for they are no enemies, but rather allies, guiding the soul towards this blessed passage. Indeed, it is said that Witches, through the aid of the alp, drude, and mara, summon such moments to lead the way to otherworldly journeys.

DE NOCTURNIS PARALYSIIS ET PORTA SOMNIORUM

f the *Benandanti* in the years of the fifteenth to seventeenth centuries, most were poor peasants, unlettered and lowly, or else vagabonds and sturdy beggars, dwelling beneath fortune's favorless gaze. Less than a third of the men of that age possessed the gift of letters, and such skill was scant found amongst the lower ranks of life. Like the witches, their knowledge reached little beyond the farmer's wisdom of the moon; astrology and natal charts were mysteries far removed from their grasp. Of exotic works, such as the *Picatrix* and Aḥmad ibn ʿAlī al-Būnī's *Shams al- Maʿārif*, they had neither hearing nor understanding.

The grimoires of Italy, France, and Germany, the *Clavicula Salomonis* and the *Lemegeton*, held no less obscurity for them, as did the Bible's sacred text, the writings of Christian mystics, or the tales of that fabled vale, Josaphat, whose meanings ever shifted with the teller's tongue. Yet, among these folk were healers, wise in their simple craft, who often memorized one or two Latin phrases of priests, turning them to charms and blessings in their own fashion. And, indeed, the clergy, in their care, taught the common people prayers humbler, suited to their station and their need.

DE VITA RUSTICA ET IGNORANTIA SACRA

nlike the grimoires of Latin and Arabic lore, wherein the conjuration of spirits is wrought with rigid form and solemn rite, the congress of the Benandanti with spirits of the otherworld and the dead is of a nature far more homely, as one might converse with a neighbour or a chance companion upon the street. A spirit may be summoned by naught save the knowing of its name and the calling thereof in words of fanciful grace or poetic craft, or by forsaking the bonds of flesh to journey forth and meet the spirit in its own realm. 'Tis held as truth that the spirits of the departed, and those beings of the unseen realm, possess a height of communion that surpasseth all mortal tongues, comprehending every language and even the silent discourse of thought unspoken.

Benandanti remedies, charms, and incantations lack the labyrinthine intricacies of other traditions, for their trust lieth in the spiritual prowess and innate might of the practitioner.

Being experienced in decades of Arabic meditations of theurgy within astrological windows of time, such as the *Shams al-Maʿārif* and its Egyptian ṣūfī practitioners, I find no superiority in these learned works despite their astrological refinements; their results, subtle and slow, pale beside the swift efficacy of the Benandanti.

Each path beareth its strengths and frailties. Ancient Egyptian *Duat* devil-summoning and Latin demon conjuration, as in the *Lemegeton*, boast rapid results and draw forth spirits of harrowing intensity, secured by sword and circle to obey the conjurer's will. The Benandanti, lacking such fierce congress, yet match the grimoires in gentler summonings where spirits show less ferocity. The craft of the Benandanti is an art profound, wherein the spirit's realm is beheld to discern the hidden workings of the world and to remedy its disorders. They tread within that unseen dimension to alter it, albeit within the limits of its nature, that fate and the material may be swayed. Less do they lean on spirits or talismans than other traditions, though such tools are not absent from their ways. Instead, their art demandeth a keen mastery of the mind and the psychic powers of the soul.

Practise moments of silence, both within and without; and if one doth struggle, turn one's mind to feel the spiritual flame that hovereth over one's head. An aid in stilling the mind is to immerse oneself in breathing in the spirit, as the Saint John of the Cross doth instruct. This breath doth yield *manna*, a *puissantia* innate to all, and may be wielded as witch-fire; yet far greater toil must one expend to bring it forth, for 'tis the virtue of Saints.

DE DONO LANGOBARDORUM

anna, by symbol, is rendered as loaves of bread, whilst witch-fire findeth likeness in wine; yet neither doth require drink nor sustenance. Know that witch-fire cannot be attained through natural striving or the awakening of senses, for it is begotten by arts unnatural, passed down through lineages, and bestowed solely by the hands of its keepers. Manna may enrapture the mind and fill the blood with the warmth of wine's intoxication, bestowing states of ecstasy and divine illumination. It granteth strength to perform miracles and openeth the soul to visions. Witch-fire may likewise achieve such marvels with greater ease, yet bringeth not the highest illumination that manna doth confer. Witch-fire is a lazier puissance, given and not earned, demanding but little toil to sustain; it lendeth strength with but scant effort.

The powers of witch-fire are wrought of human artifice and cunning, refined by countless generations of magicians, even as men do craft spirits born neither of the dead nor by nature's womb. Manna, in contrast, springeth from nature's heart and the living flesh of humankind, a bridge betwixt the mundane and the mystical, unlocking the senses to a greater awareness and awakening abilities miraculous. Manna doth engender a force that, within the mortal frame, manifesteth a physical, tangible stirring, akin to the murmurous hum of bees or the thunderous roar of a waterfall, though it is without sound. The most puissant form of prayer known to the Saints is to supplicate within the stillness of silence, whilst with steadfast breath stirring potent manna.

Behold, the lot of Saints, who, clad in sorrow, live lives of woe and meet their end as martyrs crowned with tragedy's thorny wreath; whilst witches, those errant souls, do roam as vagabonds and beggars, outcast and forlorn. Such is the common lot of those who drink deep of the spirit's rapture and turn their gaze from the fleeting lures of fleshly delight. Even the first noble founders and originators of Freemasonry, though adorned with virtue and wisdom, did struggle with the burdens of worldly fortune and the frailty of mortal flesh. The best among them, though honourable and industrious, attained not to wealth nor knew the favour of Fortune's bounteous hand. They who are most richly blessed by the bounty of the earthly realm and the treasures of material wealth, whether in this age or in the dim reaches of antiquity, are ever those born into families of wealth, do first inherit riches before they turn their minds to philosophy, religion, or the ways of spirit. Of rare exceptions there be ever a few, and lo, I count myself among their number.

'Tis true, that all are born with a hidden strength within, a *puissantia divina*, whereby miracles may be wrought, and the spirit loosed from its mortal coil without needing succour of herbs, charms, spells, spirits, manna, or witch's fire.

To be *Benandante* is to know thyself beyond the veil of what men and the world would have one be. One must be true unto themselves and thus become as one secretly 'other,' walking amongst their fellows who know not but to mistake themselves for the roles and characters the world hath bestowed upon them. One must need continue to play the parts and scripts society hath given one, yet ever hold fast to the knowledge of who one truly is beneath the mask.

For ninety-nine days must one seek a quiet place hidden within the bounds of the graveyard, there to sit offering a coin or other means of respect unto the spirits of that hallowed yard. In stillness and with silence deep within, thou art to merely observe, a means by which one may attain both the quietude of mind and the stillness of body. From this place of utter calm, one shalt behold reality as it is, and know that one art not who one hath thought oneself to be—neither thoughts, nor feelings, nor cravings, nor the fleshly form. Observe without judgment, without attachment, and without reproach the stirrings of the mind, the sensations of the flesh, and the stirrings of the heart, as though one wert a stranger housed within mortal shell. By this practice shalt one awaken to the consciousness of thy true self.

Notes of Ingress

The noble thirteenth-century mystic of the good Catholic Church, Eckhart von Hochheim, spake thus of God: a being beyond all being and a *nihilitas* transcending all existence, who doth embody a changeless essence and a nameless nothingness. Von Hochheim did also declare: when the mind is teeming with thoughts, it is bereft of God; but when the mind is emptied of all things and made open and receptive, one is full of God.

A *Benandanti* elder, a great heretic wise in years and full of grace, didst speak unto me thus: "God is a divine no-thingness, without form, without gender, devoid of personality and opinion, God is naught but the place of pure oneness."

In the year 1580, Battista Moduco did before the Inquisition aver that the practices of the *Benandanti* were absent of Christian prayers, no sign of the holy cross did they make, nor yet call upon the Saints or blessed Maria. This he spake truly. Neither the malefic spells of witchcraft, nor pacts with the devil, nor the dread use of human remains in necromantic workings are among their ways. Yet do we hear of certain *Benandanti* who perform such deeds, weaving Friulian folk magic with their craft– not as a corruption, but as an extension, for their practice imposeth no fetters upon the beliefs or acts of any individual, being unlike a religion in its nature. In the fifteenth to seventeenth centuries, the *Benandanti* were Catholic and did rise to defend Christians against witches' mischief, though their practice itself was not bound to the faith of Christ.

In the Friulian folk mysteries, there abideth a craft called *preenti*, wherein, by word of charm, by tuneful lay, or by incantation, a force is summoned to flow through the practitioner's hands, that it might heal the frail or fashion a spell. Often it is that these *preenti* are prayers of Christian devotion, serving as conduits for the might of the Christian god Himself; yet not always is this so. To undertake the rite of a *preenti*, one must first receive its sacred empowerment, conveyed by the laying on of hands, whereby the receiver is granted words of power, whose utterance unlocketh the force divine or dread, to be summoned at any moment and wielded as their own.

To be initiated, one must have seen thirteen summers or more and must be born either with a caul or be a 'talent'–the latter being one who demonstrateth gifts and abilities well suited to the path. The practices afore-mentioned are strongly suggested to be well known and familiar to the aspirant before the rites of initiation may commence. Those practices which speak of a course of ninety-nine days are most desired to be undertaken within that span preceding the initiation, that one may taste fully of the transformation which doth unfold during such sacred rites. Upon a Thursday's night must the rite of initiation be performed, beneath the waxing light of the moon, within the darkling embrace of a shadowed wood, or upon a mountain's height, or else within a church's solemn walls. A sword, the company's banner, a church's holy chalice filled with the elixir called the blood, a loaf of bread, and a and a sanctified oath-skull must lie upon the table prepared for the ceremony.

Before assembling, all shall have bathed and donned clean black garments. The chosen, after drinking the elixir and eating a morsel of bread, doth lay their right hand over the sacred oath-skull. There, an oath is sworn—loyalty unto that secret army, to serve until their fortieth year, and never to unveil the true names of either *Benandanti* or *Malandanti*. Then must the chosen receive the Lombard's gift, that they might safely take to nocturnal flights and gaze upon life's unseen realms.

ELDUR

Notes of Ingress

The witch-fire that is the Lombard's gift is thus bestowed upon the chosen: a force, an energy, driven into the body by a male and female custodian. Each doth hold the upper arm of the chosen with their left hand, while their right doth rest upon the chosen's shoulder, pressing upon the trapezius muscle over the clavicle bone. It is through this channel, the right hand, that the gift is imparted, with the incantation of the gift muttered under breath many times over. This sacred rite of initiation, reserved for Friday's eve beneath the waxing Moon, doth unfold over no less than four hours' span; it may or mayhap be thrice enacted, according to need. Once the witch's fire is received, the chosen must cease their chant, hold their tongue, keeping silent both in this world and that beyond, and lay upon their back with chervil clasped in hand, till the dawn's first light doth grace the heavens, their hearts and minds opened to immerse in the visions of heaven, hell, and the field of flowers, led to the place that's other by a spirit of the dead who whisper truths long sought. These visions, like guiding stars, bring one to the revelation of the self, illuminate the path they must tread as they embark upon their journey as *Benandante*, a steward of this mysterious path.

DE RITU INITIATIONIS ET EXERCITU SECRETO

To be a lady or gentleman of the *Benandanti* is to be a soldier in a noble host, a knight of honour, yet unlike the knights of the mortal realm, chivalrous in truest form. One maketh no excuses as to why a task cannot be done, but rather acteth swiftly and accomplisheth what must needs be.

Die not whilst departing the body in the practice of the *Benandanti*, lest one's spirit be condemned to the hereafter, to join the heathen, a furious host, forever denied the heaven and hell of Christendom. Though diverse opinions may abound, the noble Donna Florida Basili of Undine spake of beholding Sir Bartholomaeus del Ferro, Sir Valentinus Zanutti, and sundry others amidst the procession of the dead, that company known as the Furious Host or Wild Hunt. Florida professed she could discern among them who dwelt in Heaven's grace, who languished in Hell's torment, and who yet endured the trials of Purgatory. Such claim I find reasonable, for in mine own labours of exorcising haunted abodes with an elder companion, oft did my elder declare a *specter* to be bound within Purgatory's grasp, whilst others he named as suffering in Hell. Together we endeavoured to bring

65

such souls unto Heaven's light, for spirits that walk the earth in Heaven's peace trouble the living not.

Notes of Ingress

Good Donna Florida Basili, who vanished without trace before the Inquisition could deal any serious blow upon her, slipping thus from their grasp like shadow into night.

Throughout the annals of Christendom, of all the Saints who traversed the celestial heights and the infernal depths, no two accounts of these otherworldly realms bear the same likeness. Each vision standeth apart, unique unto the seer. The Vale of Josaphat, where *Benandanti* and *Malandanti* clash in spectral battle, is a prime example, for even among those present at a mystic fray, their eyes behold differing visions. One may glimpse a radiant glen, while another perceiveth a field steeped in ·shadow. These realms of the beyond share but common threads–a tapestry wherein Heaven remaineth a blissful paradise of sunlight and peace; Hell unfailingly weaveth in terrors to curdle the soul; and the Vale of Josaphat ever bloometh with resplendent flowers and roses of fair hue, sweet-scented to the senses. Thus doth each journey paint its own tale, ever shaped by the wanderer's gaze.

Even the afterlife's charts inscribed upon ancient papyri by Egyptian priests for souls departed, no two maps ever mirror one another. Each scroll beareth its own path and perils, bespoke for the journeying dead. Only the threads of common themes bind their shifting roads: the trials of the soul, the tests of the heart, and gates guarded by sacred might. Likewise, among the Sethian Gnostics, the hallowed *Liber Ieû* standeth apart from the paths inscribed in the *Pistis Sophia*. Nor do either align with the secretive paths of Jewish *Hekhalot* lore. While themes—celestial descent, radiant thrones, and holy mysteries—do interlace their tales, the way is ever unique. Thus doth the spirit's journey bend and twist, its map ever changing with each soul's quest, though the stars of destiny may be shared.

DE VISIONIBUS ALTORUM ET VALLIS JOSAPHAT

In the lore of ancient Egyptians, Arabians, and Jews, and others too, 'tis custom to commit to memory lengthy hymns of words unintelligible to any tongue, guardian names, and answers to riddles and trials that mark their passage through otherworldly realms. Also, must they traverse from seven to one-and-twenty abodes before they reach their most coveted rest. Myself and others who have walked these paths do understand: such rites are wrought to deepen the soul's immersion, to paint the visions of the otherworld with hues more vivid and grand, to fashion an ideal afterlife. Yet, I have seen how some, by overburdening with excess complexity, do but lose the enchantment they would seek to enrich. Theologians, being men of letters yet not true mystics, when they fashion spirit-maps, though their purpose be well-meaning, do often encumber them with cumbrous trifles and tasks that mar immersion. Contrariwise, the maps devised by mystics' hands are wrought with a keen eye for the essentials, fitting for a journey well undertaken. The seasoned wayfarer doth at once perceive the stark difference, and knoweth well the qualifications–and the lack thereof–that the author bringeth to such endeavours.

Notes of Ingress

The *Benandanti's* aim doth differ from these mystery traditions; for they wander not to secure the afterlife, but rather to cross into otherworlds to redeem cursed souls and turn fortune's tide in the mortal realm. Therefore, the maps lack needless complexity, and the paths are shaped by purpose and pragmatism. The more one ventureth forth, the more vivid and entrancing grow these realms of passage.

DE CLAMORIBUS DRACONUM ET SIGNIS ULTIMIS

When bestowing the Lombard's gift upon the chosen, one must align oneself truly with the ancestral power in its perfect essence; one must summon the recollection of when the power had fully ripened, coming into awareness within oneself— weeks after it was granted. It is in the revisiting of this peak experience, this wellspring of memory, that the energy flows in perfect alignment. As one doth murmur the incantation, the words forge a key of resonance, allowing the chosen to access the force whenever they chant the same words. Feel the current of power pass down one's arm, through one's palm, and into the flesh of the chosen, as the gift is thus fused unto them.

When crafting the incantation for the chosen, stray not into excessive ornamentation, for too much artifice doth please but few. The words must needs be remembered, and if the chosen be a humble soul of rustic wit, unversed in letters, then let the charm consist of but five words—one for each finger of the hand. Let these words befit the purpose, evoking that which is sacred and potent, with Godan's name among them. Thus, words simple, yet suffused with power, that the spell may be easily recalled and effectually employed.

As for the Malandanti's gift, 'tis delivered in much the same manner, though it cometh from beyond the northern Alps, carrying with it a malevolent familiar, known as Alp or Mara, a mount that doth send the witch soaring through nocturnal flights and aids in his or her witchcraft. Oftentimes, too, the Benandanti receive spirit helpers, particularly during marriage feasts attended in their night flights. Though wed to such spirits, earthly bonds with the living are not disturbed. Rare it is for men to wed spirits, yet it is far more common among women.

The power received and cultivated by the Benandanti is known as the Lombard's gift, for it sprang from the heritage of a diligent and devout Christian folk, the Lombards, who descended from beyond the northern Alps and made their dwelling in the lands of Italy.

The incantation is a summoning of the Lombard's gift, to be whispered in solitude, in chambers dim or shrouded from the light, that it may stir and rouse the ancient power. If it so please the individual, one may say it accompanying one's morning prayers. Words do differ, for each incantation beareth the mark of the custodian's choice of words and even language when the gift was first bestowed. An incantation well devised is brief and rhythmic, direct in its intent; yet, take heed, for only one divine name may be invoked within its lines–'Godan' must indeed find place among the words spoken. Who is Godan, one doth inquire? Some have claimed 'tis but a name for god in the tongue of Old High German (Old High German: *got, cot.* Germanic Lombardic: *guþ*), and verily, the ancient Lombardic speech doth bear great likeness to that venerable language. Yet, in the teachings imparted to me by an initiator and elder, Godan is more than a word or divine title; he is a human ancestor, the first progenitor of the Lombard folk, from whom Benandanti lineages sprang forth.

Yet, in the sixth century, Paulus Diaconus, himself of Lombard descent, penned in his work *Origo Gentis Langobardorum* that Godan and his lady Frea were the Germanic deities venerated by the Vandals and the Lombards during their days in Scandinavia. Due to lineage, I do cleave unto the lore that speaketh of Godan as a venerable human forebear, an ancestor whose spirit doth reside in the roots of the tribe. For traditions do shift and grow, beliefs bending like the boughs of a tree to the winds of time, shaped by the lineage that beareth them forth.

"*Est insula qui dicitur Scadanan, quod interpretatur excidia, in partibus aquilonis, ubi multae gentes habitant; inter quos erat gens parva quae Winnilis vocabatur. Et erat cum eis mulier nomine Gambara, habebatque duos filios, nomen uni Ybor et nomen alteri Agio; ipsi cum matre sua nomine Gambara principatum tenebant super Winniles. Moverunt se ergo duces Wandalorum, id est Ambri et Assi, cum exercitu suo, et dicebant ad Winniles:* "

Aut solvite nobis tributa, aut praeparate vos ad pugnam et pugnate nobiscum". Tunc responderunt Ybor et Agio cum matre sua Gambara: "Melius est nobis pugnam praeparare, quam Wandalis tributa persolvere". Tunc Ambri et Assi, hoc est duces Wandalorum, rogaverunt Godan, ut daret eis super Winniles victoriam. Respondit Godan dicens: "Quos sol surgente antea videro, ipsis dabo victoriam". Eo tempore Gambara cum duobus filiis suis, id est Ybor et Agio, qui principes erant super Winniles, rogaverunt Fream, uxorem Godam, ut ad Winniles esset propitia. Tunc Frea dedit consilium, ut sol surgente venirent Winniles et mulieres eorum crines solutae circa faciem in similitudinem barbae et cum viris suis venirent. Tunc luciscente sol dum surgeret, giravit Frea, uxor Godan, lectum ubi recumbebat vir eius, et fecit faciem eius contra orientem, et excitavit eum. Et ille aspiciens vidit Winniles et mulieres ipsorum habentes crines solutas circa faciem; et ait: "Qui sunt isti longibarbae" ? Et dixit Frea ad Godan: "Sicut dedisti nomen, da illis et victoriam". Et dedit eis victoriam, ut ubi visum esset vindicarent se et victoriam haberent. Ab illo tempore Winnilis Langobardi vocati sunt." – Paulus Diaconus, *Origo Gentis Langobardorum*, 7th century

The hue of this ancestral force that is the Lombard's gift, this spiritual fire, is either dark crimson, blue, or black, depending on the lineage. Blue or clear translucent flame signifieth a younger line, while black, dark and gleaming, marketh a more ancient survival. The intoxication from the black is as the soul of the barbarian Goths-nightmarish, somber, and haunting like a dark fairytale-its visions shadowed in an expression of sorrow. Yet the blue is more life-affirming, joyful, vibrant, a charmer, and an aphrodisiac. Either empowerment lifteth the spirit into a state of ecstasy, loosening the very soul from its mortal shell, thus awakening it to greater realms of awareness and a deeper clarity within the dreamscape. In such a state, the veil betwixt the body and the spirit world groweth thin, making the possession by spirits, and the art of mediumship, as easy as breathing itself.

The energies conferred upon a soul within these ancient rites are oft spoken of in terms of the poetic, known as the "witch's light," the "witch's fire," or even as a "draught of poetry" or "flower." Yet think not that these are fires that burn as earthly flames, nor flowers that grow from common soil. The use of "witch's fire" as a metaphor attempteth to express the intangible, to encapsulate a force that is at once elusive and potent. It mirroreth other poetic descriptions, like the Hermetic "invisible green fire" or the "smokeless fire" of the Djinn in Islamic lore, where such terms strive to capture the essence of powers beyond ordinary perception. These energies may manifest in many guises and in varied degrees of warmth or cold, and some partake more of the nature of gloom and shadow than of radiance. These spiritual fires, though unseen to the common eye, do bear a distinction most curious, for each possesseth its own unique semblance and quality. The effects do often present themselves upon the body as if they were of some tangible, quasi-physical nature, manifesting in sensations both strange and palpable. The influence upon the mind doth intoxicate as though some ethereal draught had been imbibed, sending the senses awash in otherworldly rapture. Moreover, they bring with them varied side effects and properties, like tokens of their peculiar nature. Some may leave a warmth to linger, others a chill, and some do stir the humours in ways most mysterious, affecting mood, vigour, or the very spirit's disposition. Thus, these fires are known not only by their heat or coldness but by the myriad sensations and effects with which they grace-or vex-those who dare to court their ancient flames.

Lo! The scholars and the materialists, perched upon the lofty heights of their intellect, seek to dissect and comprehend that which hath eluded their grasp. From the cold confines of reason, they endeavour to rationalise mysteries untouched by their hands or hearts. Yet, how can one speak of *elfriche* stars when they have never ventured beyond the earthly veil? Thus, their words ring hollow, like echoes in a vast and empty hall, for true understanding springeth not from mere study, but from the lived experience that animateth the soul.

All the Benandanti fires do possess the power to grant the common folk a fleeting glimpse of the shades of the departed or the phantasms of things unseen. These spiritual fires, too, bestow upon the Benandante the gifts of health, vigour, and a shield of spiritual might, akin to armour forged of unearthly force. Before one allow a spirit to possess one's body, or one venture to journey in spirit, slipping into that slumber which is not slumber, these energies must be invoked, allowing oneself to surrender and revel in their blissful ecstasy. In such a state, the soul unbindeth itself from the flesh, as if unmoored from its earthly vessel, and is set free to wander where it will. Benandanti may traverse the realms of heaven and hell whilst still in the land of the living, through the wondrous flight of the spirit unbound from flesh. The blissful ecstasies and paradises that may be tasted through such flights far surpass journeys wrought by witches' salves and ointments. While the infernal realms may indeed be accessed through the use of such baleful salves-sometimes known as magic salves or sleeping ointments-these concoctions are employed by those who, lacking the sacred gift, cannot otherwise send their spirits forth.

Among the Benandanti, the use of witches' ointments and salves was but a practice most rare, seldom employed save for scant accounts, as have been recorded. One such tale recounteth a cowherd of Latisana, who, in his dealings, was said to employ these unguents. Another tale speaketh of a woman named Menica, a courtesan from Cremona, whose path did also find occasion to resort to such potions. Thus, while not customary in the ways of their kind, these few do attest that even among the Benandanti, the craft of salves was not wholly unknown.

Yet, herein lieth a peril, for the preparation of these ointments calleth for the use of plants both poisonous and potent, combined with the more dire practices of corpse medicine. Crafting such balms demandeth precision, for each ingredient–from deadly aconite to treacherous belladonna–must be measured with utmost care. Indeed, aconite must first be applied to the mount of Venus on the palm, that any sensitivity might be tested, lest the salve bring harm. An error in this delicate balance may result in dreadful slumbers filled with fleeting, chaotic visions, or worse still, the final sleep of death. If not enough to subdue the body in the sleep that is not sleep, the unholy mixture may cause the limbs to tremble, the tongue to dry, and the wretch to fall into a stupor wherein speech and swallow fail.

The infernal sights brought by these salves would make even the frightful depictions of hell by Christian painters seem a merry scene. Those who dare seek their solace through these methods desire not a mere stupor, but the false death of the body with the mind still alert, wandering in visions akin to flight beyond the veil. Yet such practices, when indulged too often, may bring ruin upon both body and soul. And even the famed mushrooms that grant visions, or the draughts made from the urine of those who have consumed such fungus, no matter how compounded with medicinal herbs, can never equal the transcendence and ecstasy of true Benandanti flight—given by ancient empowerment and perfected through disciplined development.

Vision-inducing mushrooms or the subtle warmth of a draught may indeed serve to loosen the soul, preparing it to become a more pliant vessel for spirit possession. Yet such aids are not to be favoured when the fierce dance of battle calleth forth the warrior's trance; there, one doth best to enter the mystic fury unsullied by such potations. Those unversed in the arcane arts and the secret workings of the mind can scarcely comprehend the mastery required to attain such altered states. They do prattle that only with the crutch of strong drink, herbs, or a malady of the mind may one touch upon such ecstasies, for they lack the fortitude and discipline to uncover the greater truths. To them, the mysteries of the inner world lie shrouded, unknown and unknowable.

Like unto ourselves, even the common folk may, at times, hear a knocking at their door in the liminal moments betwixt waking and slumber, or near the fourth hour of morning. Such a sound, when heard, is not of this world but an omen, a portal to the processions of the dead. When such an hour striketh, the spirit must leave the body and pass through the door, should they wish to join this spectral host and be privy to all manner of secrets unknown to the living.

In the older custom, the Alpine masked processions, such as the *Perchtenlaufen*, do knock upon doors during Christmastide. These processions, born of older traditions, are led by dancers who originally were possessed by the spirits of the dead or by characters like Woutan and Perchte herself. To have one's body possessed by traditional characters or the departed is called *furores*, a divine frenzy through which the spirits can walk among us. Likewise, in the quiet of night, we, through our dreams, do visit their world.

In these masked processions, the dancers may perceive the voices and messages of the dead or lose themselves utterly, as their bodies become vessels for the spirits or traditional characters. Such experiences may visit the common folk, yet it is only the Benandanti and witches who possess the power to leave their fleshly vessels at will, soaring through the air to meet the dead in their own strange realms. To most, the procession of the dead may appear as shadowy figures or beasts. In the customs of Germania and Siberia, spirits of the dead, and spirits of the land like the Alp, often take on the guise of beasts, even as we may cloak ourselves in the forms of animals when our spirits travel, seeking to pass unseen and unrecognised. This is why the early masks of the Alpine processions were shaped after beasts and spectres. In later times, with the coming of the *Nikolausspiel,* these masks grew to resemble the medieval, horned visage of the Christian Devil, known by the German name *Krampus.*

As in the masked Alpine processions, such as the *Perchtenlauf,* where mock battles are waged between the fair *Perchten* and the foul *Perchten,* so do we, in spirit, engage in a similar game. Yet, our contest is fought not with earthly limbs, but with spirits freed from their flesh. The armies of the Benandanti, fair of nature and purpose, do battle against the foul-natured Malandanti. If we fight well and win the game, then the land prospereth—crops flourish, livestock thriveth, and business is bountiful. But should we falter, it foretelleth a season of possible woe, hardship, and famine.

DE ARMIS PLANTARUM ET BELLA SPECTRALIA

In these spectral wars, we arm ourselves with different plant weapons (grape vine, wheat, corn stalks, fennel, sorghum), each according to the season and the crops that reign therein. Yet, most commonly, the Benandanti wield the humble fennel stalks adverse to witches or holy viburnum rod, whilst the Malandanti brandish the sorghum stalks in their defence. The plants serve not only as arms in this spiritual conflict but also in healing, where similar battles may unfold against demons or spirits that bring sickness upon an individual.

Sorghum, that humble grain, is sacred solely to the revered Frau Holle, whose dwelling and shrine, some whisper, sitteth upon a mound of millet. In an ancient Anglo-Saxon verse, fennel and chervil are proclaimed as the blessed herbs created by Woden himself, whilst he hung upon the tree. These herbs, imbued with divine essence, it is said, serve as weapons against evil spirits, poison, grievances, baleful spells, and treacherous foes.

"Fille and Finule, felamihtigu twá,

þá wyrte gesceop witig drihten,

hálig on heofonum, þá hé hóngode;

sette and sænde on VII worulde

earmum and éadigum eallum tó bóte.

Stond héo wið wærce, stunað héo wið éattre,

séo mæg wið III and wið XXX,

wið feondes hond and wið færbregde,

wið malscrunge mánra wihta."

– The Lacnunga, codex MS Harley 585

The Wayfaring-tree, known as *Viburnum lantana*, is unlike its talismanic kin, for it is not a crop to be harvested. Rather, it is esteemed for its charms, employed to safeguard livestock against the malevolent arts of witchcraft. This noble shrub, bearing blossoms fair and fruits abundant, serveth as a protective sentinel in the pastoral realm, warding off the sinister intentions of those who might seek to harm the gentle creatures of the field.

Viburnum, fennel, garlic, beeswax, and crosses hewn of olive wood, and salt, are all employed to bless, to heal, to exorcise, and to work as bane 'gainst witches and vampires in the lore of folk.

Moreover, the stalks hold another secret—when grasped in hand during slumber, they induce a special sleep, known to the Benandanti, wherein the spirit waketh and roameth freely, fully aware, within dreams. A curious art it is, and one that doth call to mind the ancient Egyptian craft of wordless conjuration, whereby the mighty demon and god Besa is beckoned forth. The ritual commandeth thus:

Offer up a bird of flight in sacrifice—yet let it never be ibis, falcon, vulture, nor hawk—unto the goddess Auset (*Isis*), over a vessel wherein lieth a long strip of cloth. From the blood thus shed, pour a portion into a vial of *kyphi*, or wherein is mingled a potion compounded of henna, honey, myrrh, and wine infused with blue lotus, mandrake, and Syrian rue.

With this potent draught, mark upon one's left palm a rough-hewn and crude likeness of Bes. Then take the strip of cloth steeped in the sacrifice and bind it fast about the left hand; wind the remainder about one's neck, and enter both into an external and internal silence. Lay upon a rush mat, one's head near a brick of soft, unbaked clay, with a stylus upon it, to record and remember the important matters revealed in one's visions. For the cloth, hallowed unto Auset, doth shield one from the restless dead and demons that stalk the *Duat*, and it compelleth the spirit inked upon one's palm to rise forth and answer one's summons. Such is the spell entire, with naught omitted, and in its perfect enactment, it leadeth the caster into a slumber light as a feather, where dreams become as half-waking thoughts. By this wordless art of conjuration in Egyptian demonology, doth one finds audience with Bes within the *Duat*, through the realm of dreams, to sue for favour or to strike bargains in the shadowed plane.

Notes of Ingress

In the days of my youth, I did perform this rite as it was taught unto me, even as it is now set forth in these words. In that solemn hour, I beheld with mine own eyes the mighty goddess Auset and the two-dancing cat-like dwarves Bes and Beset, and in their dread presence did I feel the weight of mine own mortality, for to stand before such power is to know the peril of one's own insignificance. It was then revealed unto me that by this rite any soul might summon forth a demon of the *Duat*, inscribing upon the left palm the demon's image or hieroglyphs of the demon's name in place of Bes's likeness. And through the mighty name of Auset, might such a spirit be compelled and held in thrall. In another rite, upon my left palm did I trace the form of a baboon with the head of a dog, bearing a knife, to portray In-tep, the Egyptian guardian demon, whose wrath falleth upon intruders and thieves that move against the summoner; and thus was the fall of a young man from a great height accomplished. Likewise, in yet another rite, I did inscribe upon my left palm the likeness of a bird with a cat's head, the image of Ikenty, a guardian demon, whose grim hand wrought the end of a labourer in a travailing mishap. Each of these dread spirits did I charge with a task, commanding them in the name of Auset whilst I wandered the *Duat* through the dreamscape, shielded by a cloth stained with blood and hallowed by Auset's power; and each demon fulfilled the charge laid upon them.

Notes of Ingress

As Friulian Benandante Battista Moduco did point out, a strange and perplexing mystery doth arise: Why, in all the rites and sacred practices of the Benandanti, despite being carried out in the lands of Catholic Italy, is there no making the sign of the cross, no invocation of Maria, nor of Jesus, nor of the holy Saints?

Yet within their curious customs, nocturnal battles are held upon the Thursdays of each of the four Catholic Ember weeks. Festivals introduced by the Catholic Church, not observed by the Arian Christian nor pagan forefathers of the Benandanti. Among the Germans, these nocturnal battles were waged upon a Thursday every three months of the year, yet not in strict accord with the Ember weeks of the Church.

In Catholic Rome, originally 'twas three Ember weeks that were first hallowed in the 3rd century, before they grew into four in the late 5th century. By the 8th century, the custom had spread to the rest of Christendom. It is often theorized that the original three Ember weeks were to replace pagan Roman festivals. Germanic and Roman pagan folk would offer sacrifices during seasonal festivals to court the favour of spirits, seeking to bless their fields and flocks.

The hallowed nature of Thursdays doth owe itself to ancient pagan roots, especially in those lands north of the Alps. This day was consecrated to the Lombard ancestral spirit Donar, who ruled over tempests, thunderbolts, and the sacred arts of blessing and sanctification. A mighty spirit, he was said to have a beard of fiery red, and he found delight in the offering of goat sacrifices. Within the Germanic tribes, the observance of holy rites upon this day lent them a deeper sanctity and rendered their sacred deeds more wholesome

Donar, a protector of mankind, did bear a likeness to the Greek Hercules in his compassion and strength. Though the Christian faith spread apace, traces of ancient worship lingered long among the Lombard folk; even in the 8th century, remnants of the old ways survived, with sacrifices and veneration of pagan spirits persisting amidst those who now professed Christianity. Thus, some fragments of the elder faith found a way to endure, woven subtly into the life of Lombard descendants.

Throughout the breadth of Italy, on the second day of November, is held *Il Giorno dei Morti*, the Catholic Day of the Dead, wherein families do wend their way unto the cemeteries, bearing offerings for their departed kin. Yet, in the Alpine lore of the *Benandanti*, the dead draw yet nearer to the world of the living, for during the nights from Christmas, the twenty-fifth of December, to Epiphany, the sixth of January, the gates of the otherworld do stand flung wide.

UOTAN

Notes of Ingress

In the Ember weeks, the spectral procession of the dead doth appear and partaketh in the nocturnal battles, yet in the twelve nights betwixt Christmas and Epiphany, their presence among the living is most puissant. This season is hallowed and dreaded alike, for all beings of the otherworldly realm wield their influence more potently upon the mortal sphere; necromantic arts wax strong, and malefic magics reach their zenith. Some hold it true that the twelve nights preceding Christmas through to Epiphany be the most perilous and supernatural span of the year, a time when enchantments do abound, and danger stalketh unseen.

At this season, Godan may appear, clad all in black, riding a carriage as black as night, its wheels wreathed in flame, and drawn by steeds darker than coal, their eyes aglow with unearthly fire. Or, as a man robed in sable, he may bestride a white horse, marvellous to behold, bearing four legs—or eight—as if it were born of realms beyond mortal sight.

A *Benandanti* fellowship is a gathering of folk from every station of life, from sturdy beggars to lords of great estates, from the tender youth to the withered elder, from those outcast and forsaken to those adored and celebrated. In this company, all are treated as equals, and all may partake in their sacred assemblies and the otherworldly feasts around a walnut tree. The sacred walnut tree, in the darkened hours of night, doth stand as a shrine to the mighty *Antecessor*, Godan. 'Tis said that beneath its shadowed boughs, his form doth sometimes manifest, a faceless black silhouette crowned with a broad-brimmed hat. Beasts of shadow–ravens, serpents, and wolves alike–are sacred unto him and his consort, the fair Frea, whose omens reveal themselves in creatures of midnight hue. For both do favour the colour black, a sign of mystery and the unseen.

The procession of the dead, or the furious host, which they do lead, taketh on many forms–at times, as men and beasts of the appearance of flesh, and at others, as shadowy phantoms, dark as the very night itself. Thus, the walnut tree becometh a place where the veil betwixt worlds is thinnest, and the passage of spirits followeth the path laid by the hallowed pair, guiding the restless through realms both seen and hidden. Yet why such reverence for the walnut, one cannot say with certainty, for surely, methinks, an ash, yew, or pear tree would seem a more fitting sentinel at such a crossroads of mystery. In the matter of Godan and the walnut tree, it doth seem probable that the association sprang from rites of yore, recorded by chroniclers who spied upon the doings of the early Christian Lombards. In the sixth and seventh centuries, these Lombard warriors, stationed near the river Sabato, performed strange ceremonies round a tree of unknown *species*. Mounted on horseback, they did race toward it, and from its boughs did devour a portion of some beast's hide, though what manner of beast, we are left untold. Additionally, these soldiers are said to have worshipped a serpent effigy, but what this serpent did resemble—whether wrought of wood, metal, or some other craft—the chroniclers failed to speak, leaving it a mystery. The tree itself was said to be sacred to Godan and Frea, old Lombard spirits from pagan times. When poets and scribes sought to recall this ancient rite, they did, by assumption or invention, name the sacred tree a walnut, thus entwining that tree with the cult of Godan in Italy for centuries to follow.

Some have surmised that the serpent idol revered by the Christian Lombards might have been a representation of the goddess Isis. Yet, it is curious that the Lombards, while perhaps drawing upon certain imagery, did not observe the rituals or follow the customs traditionally associated with the Roman cult of Isis in that area, nor did they uphold its sacred taboos. Therefore, it cannot be thought that this serpent figure was the deity, Isis. Thus, the true nature of this idol may forever remain shrouded in mystery, along with the Norse *Ormgudinna* serpent-witch and dragon-lady carvings.

The sacred tree of the goddess Isis in Egypt, known as the *Ficus sycomorus*, transformeth into the *Ficus carica* when her cult findeth footing in Rome. These trees are esteemed as shrines, for in them dwelleth Isis (*Auset*), the lady of such verdant beings. Beneath their roots, the gods of the Egyptian underworld stand sentinel, and these trees serve as portals for the souls of both the living and the departed to traverse into the *Duat*, the realm where the spiritual otherworlds abide. Approached with grace and reverence, one must don white linen, be freshly bathed and anointed with perfume, to honour the sacred trees. Here, offerings of food and libations are to be laid at the tree's base, a testament to devotion and respect the Isis devotee hath for the divine presence ensconced within. Certainly not the rites of barbarous Lombard knights, who, upon their steeds, do strike with ruthless arms at the bleeding sacrifice that dangleth from the branches of a tree.

Pietro Piperno, in his *De Nuce Maga Beneventana*, did tell of how, in the seventh century, the holy Bishop Barbatus, moved by a righteous fervour, did uproot this sacred Lombard tree, that he might extinguish the flame of paganism still burning at its roots. In Germany and Italy, walnut trees are oft associated with weddings, and it is told that in the spectral feasts of the *Benandanti*, weddings do oft take place. The walnut trees were also held sacred to the rites of Greek *Caryatis*, protector of the chaste and guardian of maidenly purity. Known also as *Carya*, the Lady of the Nut-Tree, she was an aspect of the goddess Artemis, or to the Romans, Diana, whose virgin priestesses, the *caryatidai*, upheld her sacred vow of virginity. Each year, unwed maidens dressed in white danced the *Caryatis* in a festival of honour to Artemis *Caryatis*, a celebration of their virtue and her divine favour. The rites of *Caryateia* thus preserved the sanctity of virginity, celebrated with reverence beneath the shade of the sacred walnut's boughs.

When churchmen speak of a goddess beyond the bounds of Italy and Greece, whom they do name Diana or Hecate, 'tis neither of these celestial powers whom they speak. Much as the Romans called Wotan by the name of their god *Mercurius*, for Wotan doth share in the nature of a trickster and is a patron of magic, merchants, crossroads, and speech, even as *Mercurius* himself doth govern such realms–so is the confusion born. Diana, Artemis, nor Hecate share any true bond with the *Benandanti*, yet some do entwine this goddess with their name, for in the Christian ages it was said she was one of the deities that did lead the procession of the dead or *Wild Hunt*. Moreover, Maria Panzona of Latisana, an epileptic woman and *Benandante* herself, did claim to offer homage unto the Devil–perhaps Godan, or even the Christian Satan–though only to obtain witch powers to aid others and oppose malefic witches. She professed allegiance solely to Christ and recounted her presence at an otherworldly Sabbath ruled by a figure akin to a devilish abbess. Perchance 'tis the corpse-faced or skull-faced crone of the walnut tree, I have been told about, whose visage doth gleam with a pallor like unto death itself. From this mention of the devil-abbess alone arose the conjecture that Diana might be connected to the

Benandanti, yet such a link resteth upon naught but the frailest speculation.

The Inquisition, in its relentless zeal, did seize from Maria Panzona's dwelling a red powder, which she used to still the fitful seizures that did torment her. They, in their ignorance, called it flying ointment, though it was naught but a mixture with cinnabar. After a trial of far more serious accusations, they did condemn her to three years in prison and a sentence of perpetual exile from Latisana. Yet, though she endured such harshness, the Inquisition, in the fullness of time, troubled her no more. Untouched by their malice, she did carry on with her work, becoming a most powerful *Benandante*.

Churchmen have spoken of most vile and dreadful things concerning Diana, recounting reports, chiefly from Germany and some from France, that speak of witches in the goddess's thrall feasting upon infants and engaging in cannibalistic orgies. Yet, from our knowledge of the histories, it is evident such horrid deeds are in truth anathema to the customs of Diana's cult, for such actions transgress sacred taboos which the goddess herself would punish most severely. Now, if those churchmen had spoken about the cult of Dionysus, it wouldn't have been such an untruth. It is true that certain witchly traditions within Europe bear the mark of dark rites, wherein cannibalistic practices are said to linger; yet these bear no kinship to Diana, nor do they seek any favour from her. *Hexen*,

Strigae, and their ilk, in sooth, do possess a certain aversion to deities that would impose moral governance upon their craft. One can but wonder why such practitioners of the night might harbour distaste for powers that uphold laws and censure wantonness.

In ages long past, the goddess Artemis (Diana) took the form of a mighty she-bear, revered by the fierce Amazons as a deity of the hunt and protector of women, most especially young maidens. Her power and watchful eye guarded girls as they grew into womanhood. Bees and white-hued creatures became her sacred omens, while the colours of her favour, white and gold, gleamed in tribute to her divinity.

Her ancient epithets, manifold and radiant, extol her virtues: **Selasphorus**, the Bringer of Light; **Leucophryne**, the White-Bird; **Chrysothronus**, she of the Golden Throne; and **Soteira**, the Savior. Ever of virtue, she bore the names **Eucleia**, **Calliste**, the Beautiful, and **Aedoeus Parthenus**, the Revered Virgin. With shafts of gold as **Chrysalacatus**, and reins of gold as **Chrysenius**, she stood sweet-garlanded as **Eustephanus**, pure and chaste as **Hagne**, the soother **Hemerasia**, and the cherished friend of young girls as **Philomeirax**. Above all, she was **Parthenus**, the Eternal Virgin.

ORIEN

Notes of Ingress

Ancient Greek myth tells of Artemis, goddess of the hunt and protector of maidens, who did with her divine power transform a fair virgin into a walnut-tree, that she might escape the clutches of Dionysus, who in lustful pursuit sought to defile her chastity. In pity and wrath, the goddess thus preserved her purity, encasing her forever in the bark and branches of that noble tree, a silent sentinel against desire's dark advance. Thus the maid, untouched by the god's wanton hand, did find her sanctuary in nature's form, where she might stand, rooted in virtue, untouched by lustful flame. In times long past, the goddess Diana, whom the Greeks did call Artemis, was indeed a fierce custodian of chastity, and woe betide those who dared defile the hallowed precincts of her groves and temples with the sins of flesh. Chaste and inviolate was she, sovereign of the wilderness and guardian of virtue, who did abhor the taint of carnal impurity within the bounds of her sacred rites and sanctuaries. Whosoever transgressed against this sacred ordinance faced the grim visitation of pestilence, famine, or other grievous afflictions, sent as tokens of her divine displeasure.

Her devotees, no less than those who partook in her sacred rites, were bound by the same covenant of purity, and it was enjoined upon them to uphold this high standard within their very households. In those pagan times, young maidens who dedicated themselves to Diana's service were kept untouched by the hands of men until the hour of their espousal, that they might align themselves with the goddess's virtues of modesty and chastity. Thus was the sanctity of Diana's worship maintained, unsullied by the corruptions of mortal desire, lest her wrath be stirred to punishments most dire.

Diana, in the Roman lore, is known not merely as guardian of chastity and faithful monogamy but as the fierce huntress who, in the Middle Ages, led the spectral Wild Hunt in Italy. Her procession, fearsome and divine, stormed the heavens; yet more often, this furious host was said to be led by spirits of Germanic birth.

In her prime estate of Grecian lore, Artemis, chaste huntress and guardian of the untamed wilds, bore no claim upon the realms of death, nor held dominion over the shades of the departed. Her power did preside over the living, safeguarding the wilderness, the birth-chamber, and the purity of maidens, a force of life and nature's unbridled essence. Thus was she enshrined as the preserver, dwelling not in the shadow of the grave, but in the midst of verdant life.

Yet, when her likeness did cross unto the lands of Rome and was therein fashioned as Diana, her sphere did stretch to encompass the borders 'twixt this life and the hereafter. In her guise as **Trivia**, goddess of the three-way crossroads and sepulchral grounds, she did come to haunt those liminal spaces where boundaries fade, where the veil grows thin, and the pathways betwixt the worlds do meet. As the moon's pale mistress, her rule did extend to the ebb and flow of that celestial orb, whose waxing and waning mirrors the passage 'twixt light and darkness, life and the underworld.

Lo, **Trivia**, Diana's oldest epithet, she who reigns in Roman lore, does hold dominion over the mystic arts, divination, the sable night, and realms beneath the earth. Her sway is felt at the threefold crossroads, where diverging paths do meet and mortal fate hangs in the balance. A keeper of secrets and embodiment of an ethereal beauty, she stands apart from **Hecate**, the Greek enchantress, whom many do mistake her for. Yet in visage, she appears as a fair virgin maiden of youthful grace, adorned with an allure that charms both gods and men.

To the ancient Etruscans, **Trivia** was ever regarded as a benevolent and nurturing deity, embodying the virtues of a maternal guardian who did preside over the rites of childbirth and the well-being of the household. Her watchful eye extended to the sanctity of familial bonds, blessing the growth and prosperity of kin. Thus, she was not solely a goddess of crossroads and night, but also one whose care did encompass the life-giving mysteries, a protector of hearth and home, fostering the continuance of life with her tender ministrations.

When the moon is full, and **Trivia**'s Night does arrive, her votaries convene at such enchanted crossroads, bearing gifts of victuals, libations, and fragrant incense to gain her blessing and ward off her wroth. Another solemn rite they do perform is known as the Deipnon, a repast laid forth at the month's end. This offering, given on the eve when the moon *hath* waned to darkness, does serve to placate her and temper any ill humour, thus ensuring her favour throughout the waxing lunar tide. Through these devotions, her followers pay homage to her mysteries and seek to dwell in harmony with her divine influence.

The hues of the bright yellows of saffron-dyed cloth are most sacred to **Trivia**, like the aura and radiance of old world Hekate. Traditional offerings made unto her encompass foods often given to the shades of the departed, such as small cakes, cloves of garlic, leeks, onions, raw eggs, fish, wine, and milk. As with the goddess Diana, her most revered tree is the cypress, a symbol entwined with the mysteries of life and death, whose dark and mournful boughs whisper of her dominion over the underworld.

In the olden days of pagan worship, Trivia never did lead a procession of the dead, yet reigns as Queen of death's domain and ruler of the underworld's darkened court. To seek her counsel, one must first lay an offering at the cemetery gate, then walk among the graves in the dark hours, with a hound to lead the way. When the dog doth bark, know then a spirit draws nigh–its form a vessel through which the goddess doth see and hear, for she useth the ghost's eyes and ears as her own.

Speak then, and one's words shall be known to the goddess herself. If one *art* gifted with the gift of clairvoyance, she may reply through the tongue of that restless shade, as if her voice were breathed from the very darkness of the grave. Thus, through such rites may one commune with **Trivia**, Queen of the dead, and glean the secrets kept within the shroud of night.

Trivia is the guide within the darkest hour, the beacon when no star doth shine, leading those who wander through night's veil, where all else is dark and light is naught.

Italian Taranta rituals and the dance of Pizzica bear no bond with Diana, for they spring from the roots of Dionysian rites, brought forth from Greece. Yet the Tammurriata, that too of ancient Dionysian heritage, may serve to summon spirits of the departed or deities, whether they be Diana, Trivia, or of any other neighbouring European land's lore, to commune or take possession to seize the dancer's mind, making of them a vessel for voices beyond the grasp of common folk.

As those who perish in the masked procession dances of Austria and Bavaria, so too, those who meet their end in the Benandanti's nocturnal battles are forbidden from being laid to rest in Christian graves. Neither Heaven nor Hell may claim their souls, for their spirits must evermore walk with the procession of the dead as Malandanti. Paulo Gasparutto didst speak unto the Inquisition thus: 102 whosoever parts from the body, journeying as the Benandanti for the space of four and twenty hours before returning, shall find their spirit sundered evermore from fleshly form. And once the body be laid to rest, such a spirit shall wander the earth and be known as Malandante, consuming the younglings.

Witches and vile spirits of the dead, who in their ghostly forms are known to siphon the life-force from mortals to amass power and lengthen their days, do greatly favour the life-force of children, for it is untainted and purest of essence. Yet, the belief that a spirit's parting from the body for four and twenty hours leads to lasting severance is not universal among the Benandanti, though amongst some it finds credence.

Benandanti are never truly refused passage to Heaven nor to Hell. For to them, Heaven is but to dwell in a pleasant vision, and Hell, the dark prison of foul dreams. Through their noble craft, they descend to Hell, redeeming lands, crops, and souls entrapped in nightmarish realms, lifting them up to Heaven's grace. Often the living Benandanti do pray whilst in Heaven, which to them is made of visions sweet and waking dreams of paradise. Of much renown is the Benandante *Paolo Gasparutto* , who now resideth strong and with power in Heaven and is always a joy to speak to whilst in prayer.

Paolo Gasparutto was far too charming for the Inquisition to lay upon him the weight of cruel punishment. His chastisements were but excommunication and threats thereof, and he was bid to offer prayers of penance, yet naught more. Yet he, unscathed, did live his days in wealth and mirth, a man of great power, a true and noble **Benandante**, his soul untroubled by their ill designs.

To the **Benandanti**, the borders between the living and the dead are thin indeed. When we do leave our mortal frames, we behold the world not as it doth appear unto our earthly sight. Nay, the veil is lifted, and we gaze upon a realm hidden to the waking eye. It is as though the spirit, unchained, doth perceive the truths buried beneath the surface—revealing the unseen forces, the subtle spirits that dwell in every place, and even within the hearts of men. This vision, more potent than mortal sight, doth diagnose the secret workings and mysteries concealed by the guise of common reality.

There be places where the spirits of the dead do dwell, where one may feel a breeze arise from no earthly source. These wandering souls often gather about the boundary stones that mark the edges of properties, as though drawn by some ancient pull. Likewise, ancient deities, once worshipped by barbarians and Romans, are said to linger still in those places where men, in times long past, offered sacrifices in pursuit of worldly favour and fortune. One seeth many spirits in the landscape and around the various haunts when travelling in spirit. If the soul's eyes should behold such spirits, then one may find speech with them, for they are open to discourse.

When we leave our flesh and wander in spirit, the holy churches seem barren, bereft of the presence of angels or saints. Yet within, one may find the spirits of Christian souls, long departed, some who have lingered through the ages, still kneeling in prayer, their gaze fixed toward Heaven, yearning evermore for its gates to open unto them. Strange creatures do oftentimes appear, haunting mountain passes, the deep woods, and rivers, such as ogres, nymphs, and faeries, who dwell beyond the ken of mortal sight.

In ancient days, hunters did dream of beasts, and in their dreams, they did hunt and take the shape of such creatures, as their spirits did travel through the realm of slumber. Yet 'tis perilous for one's soul to assume the form of a stag and run with the deer, though such be the hunter's craft, rooted deep in times before memory or record. For by strange mischance, folk may, in their folly, see the spirit's guise as flesh, and in their ignorance, they might strike, as though one wert but a common deer of flesh and blood.

The ancestors of the Benandanti are the Lombards, a people first known as the *Winnili*, their name bearing the meaning of wolves. The Lombards were wont to take the guise of wolves, roaming the wilds or falling upon their foes. Yet, to wander as a wolf through rural villages or the bustling cities, whether by day's fair light or night's dark shroud, is ill-advised. Thus, we don other forms, that our passage be unmarked in this world or in realms beyond. Most often, we choose the guise of small birds, cats, mice, or creatures more delicate–be they butterflies, moths, or humble insects.

When once we step beyond the confines of the body, to don another shape is but an act of will, though the Egyptians, in their ancient *Books of the Dead*, do prescribe verbal incantations for such a craft. Yet, in the combat of spirits, when witches are our foe, it may avail us to assume a guise more dreadful, the form of a mighty beast, or to stand in the semblance of man, that we might meet them blow for blow.

In the dark and slumbering hours, one may beat upon a drum, summoning forth the spirits of **Benandanti**, both the living and the dead, to gather at a place and join one in battle. One doth know when this action hath prevailed, for there shall come a moment where many spectral winds do rush past, as if borne upon the wings of spirits unseen. When the spectral winds do arrive, lay oneself down as one who lieth dead, and let one's spirit part from flesh, to join the assembled host upon the field of battle. Thus, doth a captain commence the battle for his district on the Thursdays of the Ember Weeks, casting forth a net invisible that draweth within it all opposing forces. By some faceless and overpowering force, mysterious and unseen, their spirits are compelled to appear upon the battlefield, that place poetically named the *Prado di Josophat*, elsewise known as the *Field of Judgment*, where fallen warriors partake in the raptures of battle's dance, yet find no lasting death to claim them, and witches revel in what Churchmen do name as sabbats, and the walnut tree but one portal to this meadow of the folk.

DE CULTU ARBORE NUCIS ET DEORUM ANTIQUORUM

Upon this field of battle, a realm unearthly, dost lie–a narrow vale where roses in their multitude do bloom. This valley resteth betwixt a realm of darkness and a realm of light. To the sinister side, a feasting hall within a graveyard standeth, and within its bounds, the very gates of hell do yawn from an empty tomb. To the dexter side, another feasting hall in a burial ground doth rise, wherein an empty tomb doth lie–a passage through the underworld to the heavenly gates.

All these things do move and work as they were ordained, by virtue of the empowerment given at initiation, and by the memories and mysteries writ within the very force itself. To hold battles on the Ember weeks is not a necessity beyond the bounds of Friuli; yet the Thursdays make such deeds sacred and blessed, lending a noble purpose to the strife. Nonetheless, the chosen days for war must be agreed upon and known to all who would march in one's army.

The Malandanti, be they devils or witches, enter not of their own volition into the field of battle, nor do they elect their captain. Rather, they are summoned by the force of a mysterious ancestral spell, which doth also empower the fellowship of the Benandanti, both living and dead. For the Benandanti, however, the call to arms is answered through a pledge made by each to serve as guardians of the district until the age of forty. These Benandanti stand as the watchful town guard, defenders of the community's welfare. If the witch doth neither sleep nor stray beyond her mortal form upon the Ember Thursdays, nor in the hours following those sacred nights, she shall find herself not drawn unto the field of battle. By such craft, the witch may elude the summons and escape the fray. Ghosts and devils are not as the living, for they possess no body of flesh to anchor their location; thus, they cannot escape being caught in the nocturnal battles. Only witches, devils, and imps, whose curses lie upon the season's crops and livestock, shall find themselves appearing upon the battlefield. At times, curses and troubles not of a supernatural nature shall take shape as fearsome beings upon the battlefield, as though the very ills themselves were given monstrous form, to wage war with the Benandanti. Battista Moduco spake unto the Inquisitor, recounting thus: upon reaching their twentieth year, they were summoned by the sound of a drum, whose beat called forth soldiers to array themselves for battle. At this summons, their spirit would sever from the body and take flight to the assemblies. Oftentimes, these gatherings numbered near five thousand souls, some known to one another, others strangers. Yet all Benandanti did fight as one, united in their faith in Christ, whereas the enemy Malandanti fought for the Devil.

Moduco spoke of the men who served as captain, remaining in command of the company until his fortieth year. At that time, the captain was a man of eight-and-twenty, of great stature, his beard red as flame, noble in bearing. His banner was silk, of a gold lion rampant upon a field of white. In contrast, the Malandanti bore a silk banner of crimson, upon which four black devils were depicted. Their captain was a man fat and ugly, bearded in black, hailing from the German nation.

Battista Moduco, a man of subtle craft, known to most as *Gamba Secura*, a public crier by trade, did fall afoul of the Inquisition's gaze. They did decree that he should serve six months in prison for his deeds; yet, upon further counsel, they did relent and declare that he need not be confined to the dank walls of a cell, so long as he prayed and swore never to leave town.

Spirits, with tongues divine or infernal, may speak through the living, whether angels, ancient gods of forsaken faiths, the souls of the departed, demons, prophets of the sacred Scrolls, or Christ Himself. The Lombard's gift doth grant the faithful to loosen their spirits, whether seated or standing, in states of rapture and ecstasy, that such possessions may be made manifest. It often beginneth with an invocation, rich in poetic verse, calling forth the one whose spirit one doth seek to claim, until their presence, like a mead of poetry, doth intoxicate the soul. Then, in blissful surrender, the seeker doth yield to the spirit's sweet intoxication, till the mind doth adopt its nature and, through body and voice, the possessed doth move and speak, unto a humble gathering of witnesses. In mine own experience, the strength of the Benandanti lieth not in folkish charms nor simple remedies; nay, therein lieth their weakest craft. The Benandanti excel most in shaping the mortal realm through deeds wrought and visions gleaned whilst venturing into the realm beyond.

PART IV

MAZZERISME: THE DREAM-HUNTERS

A Treatise on Death's Chosen Oracles

(Herein unfolds the dread account of the Mazzeri-the dream-hunters of Corsica-whose nocturnal visions mark the doom of souls, and whose path through shadow and sleep binds them to a power vast, formless, and unseen, by which fate itself is wrought.)

The *Mazzeri* be dream hunters, who within their slumbers pursue wild beasts as oracles, foretelling the doom of mortals fated to perish on the morrow or within the passing year. In such visions, a *Mazzere* might give chase to an animal with weapon in hand, or as a predatory beast, hunting its prey. Yet 'tis not till the quarry lies dead that the hunter doth behold the face of a known individual. Inevitably, to the hunter's horror, the face of the victim will eventually be a loved one or blood relative.

To be *Mazzere* is to live in a dark faerytale, a ghost story. Oftentimes, these oracles take not the form of hunts, but unfold as portents of tragic accidents, wherein those known to the seer meet their fateful ends. In the dream world of the *Mazzeri*, I once trod a lone path, and as I passed by a lady, some unseen force did overtake me. Before I could reckon what had passed, the lady lay bleeding before me, and I stood, bloodied knife in hand. Three days following, that same woman, who was seen in the dream, did meet her fated end, far away, in a grievous accident.

DE VENATIONE SOMNIORUM

When one is alone in the *Mazzeri's* dreamscape, wandering through the wilderness, seek out a stream or flowing watercourse, for surely it shall guide one to the quarry. Once the prey doth appear, give chase, wheresoever they may flee, until one's hand doth deliver the fatal or wounding blow. If one be joined by a band of *Mazzeri*, follow their lead in pursuit of the victim. The weapon shall appear as if conjured–a gun, a bow, a spear, or perhaps a knife. Yet if no such tool come to one's grasp, take up a stone or a branch to serve as a club.

Should one find oneself wandering in unfamiliar and non-traditional landscapes within the *Mazzeri* realm, seek still the paths of water, for where streams flow, prey oft doth reveal itself. Wander until the quarry maketh known its presence, and swiftly pursue. Be forewarned, not every strike one maketh shall bear the full weight of that mysterious unseen power. Yet, even without it, one's blows shall cause pain, deal injury, or even bring death. But when that power doth seize control, one is but a vessel–naught but a glove upon its hand, wrought for boundless destruction. Until that moment, one fighteth as any *Hexe* or *Benandante* might, but when the force commandeth, one becometh the very agent of fate itself.

DE VICTIMAE CAEDE ET CARNIS PARTICIPATIONE

To kill a man, like Hexen do, through an aggressive act done in visions of slumber or states of reverie, doth require the dream-world to possess a certain intensity and depth.

When the prey lieth slain, whether it be man or beast, set thy hands to butcher, and feast upon the flesh with whatsoever tools do manifest at one's side. Oftentimes, a cauldron doth appear, bubbling over a fire, preparing the meal for one's consumption. Perchance, that great and ominous force which doth govern this shadowed realm shall prefer one to feast upon the flesh uncooked. Yet, if one possesseth the gift, one can assume the form of a beast, and partake as the wild creatures do, devouring as nature itself demandeth. But beware—if the meat doth reek with foul stench or feeleth corrupted to one's touch, know it to be diseased. Such flesh should not be consumed, but left to rot where it lieth, a warning to the wise that not all spoils are fit for the feast.

Those fated to meet death not by the ravages of disease provide bounteous feasts before death claimeth them, bestowing upon us great power when we partake of their flesh in the dream-state after a kill. This ghastly repast alloweth their spirits to journey forth in death, freeing them from the bonds of this mortal realm, preventing those souls from becoming trapped when the body breatheth no more.

DE ORIGINE TIMORE ET SPIRITIBUS AQUARUM

This phenomenon, it may have begun from humble beginnings, a mere dream-omen in some long-forgotten age. Yet, as time unfurled its course, it did gather force, and folk built a tradition around it. Thus did it merge, as one, with witchcraft and the already potent *cultus mortuōrum*. Corsicans of pre-history, a culture consumed by hunting–it was their main food source, hunting year-round. In my childhood youth, my father was an avid hunter; we were always boar hunting. It doth start to bleed into one's dreams, as any task of mundane constancy in the wake. There is a common silent fear that haunteth the back of the hunter's mind–that of killing a human in a hunting accident. One could see how this latent fear could give shape to omens of misfortune. In days of yore, hunters were guided in hunts by spirits of their dead forefathers.

Natural pools, rivers, and lakes, like dreams of the wake and slumber, serve as portals–windows unto the underworld, where spirits of the dead do dwell. In Europe's pagan past, such places were honoured with offerings and sacrifices; at times even human lives were given. 'Tis no marvel then, that throughout fair Europe do spirits haunt the waters, such as the Näcken or Nix of the

Northern lands, and the Rusalki of the Eastern lands. In far-off lands of the Orient they call them Nāga, who, with their beguiling allure, draw the living to their watery graves. These pagan spirits, timeless in their haunting, even centuries into Christendom's light, possess the dancers in folk processions, as seen in the Rusallias of Serbia, much akin to how the tribal spirits in far-off Africa claim their dancers in ritual possession. By placing offerings within the stream's bed to these spirits, one may summon forth the rain and stir the tempestuous storms to rise.

In states awake in dream and in dreaming awake, the dead find their voice, speaking truths, or perceived truths, to those who dare listen. In such states of reverie, we walk the threshold of that otherworld–a shadowed realm that doth shape and command the world we, the living, inhabit. To me, these mysteries are as clear as the waters themselves, but what doth confound the mind is the faceless, unseen force–an ominous and unstoppable power–which doth overcome and possess the hunter in fleeting moments, seizing their will to its own purpose. We are but puppets when that entity steps in; maybe it is not an entity, but the many hands of the dead.

To some, Mazzerisme be naught but a mystical affliction, a fell disease they have caught, which they suffer and endure without desire to foster its growth. They seek not to cultivate its strange powers. Yet others deem it an art—a divine boon, granting them gifts most wondrous, and insight into realms unseen. This peculiar affliction may pass from one's kin by blood; yet more often, 'tis by the intrusion of a *Mazzere* into one's slumber, where they lead the dreamer on a hunt, that the affliction is passed. Within the dream, the dreamer doth follow, until the mystical bond is forged, and thus, the gift or curse is conferred through that spectral chase.

DE SIGNADORIBUS ET MAZZERIS: OPPOSITIONES SACRAE

azzeri, in many respects, are beheld as standing in stark contrast to the *Signadori*, who serve as village healers. Where the *Signadori* ply their arts to prolong life and restore health, the *Mazzeri* traffic in the shadowy realms of death and tragic prophecy. Thus, they seem as two opposing forces: one to heal, the other to unveil the end.

A *Signadora* is of a more ancient Christianity, truer in its essence, and imbued with a faith profound and unshaken. Hers is the Christianity of yore, unblemished by the world's decay, a sanctified flame burning bright in purity and sacred devotion, unmarred by the fleeting fashions of lesser times.

Many *Mazzeri* profess the Catholic faith, yet it is not requisite for a *Mazzera* to be bound by religious belief or to hold in reverence any deities.

The *Signadori* of Corsica, well-endow'd with a great wealth of knowledge in charms and Christian prayers. Not a woman among them under the age of forty, for their wisdom and skill are wrought by the labour of many seasons. These venerable women, by their craft, do prolong the span of life and bestow health; they clear away the rain-clouds to ease the shepherds' toil. The *Mazzeri*, by contrast, may begin their path at any age, be it in the dawn of youth or in the winter of their days. To become one of their number is akin to the frightful tales of werewolves and vampires, for not by the bite of fang nor scratch of claw do they transform, but rather through the invasion of dreams by one already afflicted with the dark gift. *Mazzeri* stand as oracles of death and harm—causing it in some cases, though more often foretelling it. They possess a strange kinship with water and with the restless spirits that dwell within rivers, lakes, and natural pools. Opposite to the *Signadori*, it is the *Mazzeri* who summon forth the rain, commanding the waters by their mystic power.

DE POTENTIA AQUARUM NOCTISQUE

The *Mazzeri*, by nature, are ever stronger when near fresh waters–their strength quicken'd by rivers, lakes, or streams–and when the skies doth weep in rain, their power riseth even more. Under the shroud of night, they are most formidable, surpassing the feeble powers of day. Yet most deadly are they when entranced by slumber, or caught within a dream-like state; for in such realms, where the line betwixt flesh and spirit is thin, their dominion is absolute, and their touch, lethal.

DE CATHARINA BASTIENSI ET ANTIQUITATE MAZZERISMI

hough many do claim the *Mazzeri* to be of ancient origin, the first recorded *Mazzera* in history doth appear in the trial of a redheaded woman, the occultist Catarina of Bastia, in the year 1617. A widow, she dwelt in dire poverty and led a band of three other widowed women. Catarina seems to have been a *Signadora*, a healer of the village; a *Surpatora*, a witch who feasteth upon life's essence; and a *Mazzera*, a bearer of death's omen. She also practised the magics drawn from Solomonic grimoires. *Mazzerisme* is often deem'd ancient, for it beareth the guise of a craft from far more primal times, and its potency is such that many do take it as proof of a tradition of great antiquity. Though it doth share strong kinship with the *Benandanti* of Northern Italy, it remaineth unique among European spiritual arts. A nameless, faceless, formless, colourless, and inexorable force doth seize upon its practitioners, stripping them of their own will, compelling them in dreams to slay those whose fate, we assume, hath already been seal'd by death's decree. The force that possesseth the *Mazzeri* seemeth ancient, like unto a vast and primeval entity, bereft of any human trait, yet endow'd with an intelligence of its own— a presence that liveth and breatheth with its own will. It doth call to mind the enigmatic power that sweepeth up the contenders in the clashes 'twixt *Benandanti* and *Malandanti*, drawing their spirits forth and compelling them to appear upon the ethereal battlefield of the otherworld.

DE ELIGENDIS NOVITIIS ATQUE INITIO NEXU

Who can be Mazzeri, what we look for.

Hath the person, perchance, a keen sense of the spirits of the departed? Do they possess strange sights and perceptions beyond the common senses?

Hath the individual beheld any foretokenings of that which yet draweth nigh, whether in the realm of slumber or through waking visions, as portents of the future?

Whilst lying abed with eyelids fast shut, hath the individual found their soul and sight to wander beyond the fleshly bounds of their frame, as though loosed from mortal coil to traverse afar?

Are their dreams most frequent, a nightly happening with full recall, clear as crystal in morning's first light?

Is the individual outcast, or held in scant affection by the living and the world at large?

Doth the individual bear upon their brow the weight of melancholy, or show signs of a somber disposition?

Once the novice hath been chosen, their initiation doth commence, withal their assent being first sought. The vow must be made, sacred and binding, that never shall the names of their fellow *Mazzeri* pass their lips to mortal ears.

Most do undertake the rite of ingress at the fourth hour of the morning, when darkness yet clings to the earth's bosom and dawn's herald is but a promise. Yet, more godly Corsican folk do strive to accomplish the same upon the sacred eve of Christ's Nativity, for on that night doth god Himself decree that no evil may trespass into the world. Such is the hour when malefic forces are held at bay, and these devoted seekers place their faith in the sanctity of the moment, trusting that their rites may unfold under heaven's untainted gaze.

The soul of the hunter doth depart their mortal frame and travel to the slumbering novice's body. As the witches, known as *Vampir* or *Hexen*, do enter the bodies of others when they feed, so too doth the hunter's soul enter the novice's being, feeling the warmth as it shrinketh down to fully submerge within the blood and belly of the novice. The hunter, through intent alone, mergest with the novice's dreaming mind, and thus it cometh effortlessly to seize dominion over the realm of the novice's dreams.

In that strange realm where dream weaveth fate, the hunter doth lead the novice on a spectral chase. Often is the quarry the spirit of one departed, a kinsman who lingereth still in *Purgatorium*, yet often as well doth fate's capricious hand turn, and the hunted becometh a soul among the living. A fortunate chase revealeth but the omen of an injury to one known. Upon waking, the novice must recount what only the dream could reveal, thus sealing their infection with this dark gift.

Yet the curse taketh root fully when, in their first true *Mazzeri* dream, they find themselves gripped by an unseen force, compelled to take life or render harm. Such is no ordinary dream; it is a moment of dread clarity, when the soul doth awaken to its grim purpose, unmistakable in its truth. The gift beareth with it a tether to some vast and nameless entity, whose face none may glimpse, whose form none may fathom. This force, unseen yet ever-present, doth seize the dream-hunter at the crucial moment, overmastering their will and guiding their hand. It is this unfathomable power that delivereth the fatal blow unto their quarry, making of the hunter but a vessel through which the unknown doth act. Such is the burden of the gift, to be both wielder and weapon of a force beyond mortal understanding.

In fellowship amongst the Mazzeri, there reigneth but true equality and unfeigned solidarity. No man nor woman among them beareth the weight of outcast, nor do the follies of the world without - its prejudices and vain distinctions - take root in their company. Thus, in their fellowship is found a harmony unspoiled by the sins of common society.

We teach the Mazzere not merely to glance upon strangers, but to scry, to gaze through them. In this wise, one doth learn to discern the ill-fated souls that tread in our wake; it is those who have potential of appearing in our *Mazzerisme* dream-world, and only those marked by death. Thus, it is wise to grow a little acquainted with the doomed, for only those with familiar faces shall grace our hunts.

If one doth dwell in lonely solitude, with but scant and fleeting discourse with fellow souls, then shall their *Mazzerisme* seldom stir forth hunting dreams. For it doth draw only from those few known to the Mazzere, whose fated hour hath come, or in their times of tragedy; and with no others to claim, silence doth reign in the realm of sleep. There is always the joining of an hunting party, partaking in their shared chase–but alas, such gatherings grow scarce in these latter days.

One may indeed step into the Mazzeri dream-world even whilst dwelling within waking hours. To traverse this path, one must summon forth the spirit of a departed Mazzere, one whom one hath seen within the Mazzeri dreams. Should their name be unknown, call upon the word *Mazzera* if she be a woman, or *Mazzeru* if he be a man, yet do so with steadfast intent, invoking the precise spirit one doth remember from a Mazzeri dream.

Speak these words aloud with one's physical voice whilst the body resteth, and one's eyes be shut, to bring oneself unto a state of vision. When the spirit doth appear, entreat them to cast the *Mazzeri Net*, a spell by which they shall open the way to the Mazzeri dream-world, allowing one to enter. Yet be forewarned: no prey shall manifest in that world unless fate hath marked a soul for injury or death. If one is joined by companions in an hunting party, the dream casteth a far bigger net.

We are not as the *Surpatori* or *Hexen*, those who would become executioners of men for their own ends. Instead, we take what is given by the hands of fate, gleaning from corpses like vultures circling the dying, awaiting that inevitable fall into the grave. When the ill-fated do not arise in our dream-hunts, be assured they shall appear in the dreams of another *Mazzerè*, oft in the form of some beast, unrecognised as human until the fatal stroke reveal their true shape.

Cultivators of the Mazzeri gift, with their mystic arts, do scry over bodies of life-giving water, seeking communion with the spirits that dwell therein. These spirits, dwelling in lakes and rivers, are our allies, our teachers. Oft do they enter our dreams, gifting counsel, whispering secrets from beyond the veil.

When the creature slain is revealed to be one who hath already crossed death's threshold, it marketh that the chain binding their soul to this world is broken, allowing their ghost to depart finally unto the next life.

The disembodied voice of Catarina of Bastia, speaking through a possessed medium, doth reveal unto us that a second initiation is bestowed by the Mazzeri dead upon the living – a dark and viscous substance with which they do feed the initiate and anoint their form. Coal-black it is, akin to the shadowed essence that underlieth the otherworld of *Mazzerisme*. This dark blessing bestoweth the power to be unshackled from all evil, to transcend the very notion of sin, to walk without guilt, and to stand ever blameless within the halls of the dead. It granteth freedom from a heavy heart and from grief's oppressive weight, and looseth one from the snares that ensnare and bind the dead within dreams and haunts.

Before Catarina didst turn to the occult sciences and witchcraft, she was born unto poverty, bereft of living kin. In later years, her husband and two children met a most mysterious death. Among the poorest of the poor, she was constrained to toil in hard labour, her sole recompense mere sustenance and lodging. Thus, an empowerment that might unshackle the soul from the weight of grief and a burdened heart wouldst be a most coveted boon for one in her plight. Yet, such a boon is most fitting for those who must tread the grim path of the *Mazzeri*, beholding in the dreamscape their own hand bring death upon beloved ones, whose physical end doth swiftly follow thereafter.

Notes of Ingress

The chronicles of yore do relate that Catarina, though enshrouded by accusations most dire–of murderous sorcery and dark enchantments–served but a scant few weeks in prison's confines, sharing her fate with three other widows stricken by poverty's cruel hand. The Inquisition, for all its dread authority and thirst for accusations of witchery, did curiously fix its stern gaze upon but one charge–a love spell, deemed worthy of their singular scrutiny. Following her brief sojourn in captivity, Catarina did slip from the tapestry of recorded history, leaving naught but silence in her wake.

Rest thou now in power and strength, Catarina, one's spirit haunting the winding waterways and shadowed forests, wherein the *Mazzeri's* dreams weave their sombre and spectral paths.

Rumours do whisper of a *Mazzeri Salvadori*, saviours of souls, who wander the *Mazzeri* dream-world in search of the sick and afflicted, there to heal or rescue them. Yet such a thing doth seem hard to grasp, for though a *Mazzeru* may hunt and slay of their own free will, the mightier force of wounding and death doth not come from their hand, but from a power beyond themselves. This higher power in the *Mazzeri* realm saveth not by prolonging life, but by freeing souls from their earthly cages and chains. Thus, *Mazzerisme* is no bloodthirsty sport, but a sacred rite, fulfilling its destined part in the grand scheme of life.

133

DAIMONOS

DE MANDRACHE: BELLA INTER VICOS

In days of gone by, Corsica saw fierce contests known as *Mandrache*, wherein *Mazzeri* of neighbouring villages would assemble for battle. Yet now, their numbers being greatly thinned, these clashes have fallen to memory. Each village's *Mazzeri*, led by a chosen captain, would muster their force and, from the dark hours of July's end till the first rays of August's dawn, engage their rivals. The mountain passes, marking the borders of their territories, often served as the fields of battle. By some ancient spell, the victorious village would enjoy fewer deaths till the next battle, that doth commence on the shadowed end of October, till the first light of November. During the battles, the villages would light a fire, called the *focu di i Mazzeri*, to guide the returning *Mazzeri* home to the village. Villagers would also place vessels of water by the windows, for the processions of the dead, being the Corsican Summer and Winter days of the dead–akin to the *Benandanti's* nocturnal battles, accompanied by processions of the spectral wild hunt.

In more traditional settlements, these battles were less perilous, for they chose to wield magical ceremonial weapons, akin to those employed by the Northern Italian

Benandanti. Yet, unlike their northern counterparts, whose stalks symbolised crops and fertility, the *Mazzeri* chose weapons not of the harvest, but of death itself. They bore the asphodel stem, a flower steeped in the lore of the dead, planted upon graves in the days of yore. For the *Mazzeri's* conflict was not for bounty or wealth, but to diminish the toll of death upon their village in the year to come, marking their struggle with the weight of mortality itself.

Asphodel, a symbol of death, hath its root in the ancient lore of Greece. Yet, the strange use of magical plant stems as weapons in battles of the spirit doth seem to spring from the invading barbarian cultures. Keeping an asphodel stem in one's hand's grasp during slumber doth maintain a wakeful alertness in dream.

To name these battles *Mandrake* remaineth a mystery, for no living *Mazzere* preserveth knowledge of its use, whether magical or medicinal. Traditional flying salves, ill-suited for such battles requiring wits to fight out of body, 'tis highly perilous. Their compositions boast deadly poisons, deliriums, and corpse medicine: mandrake, belladonna, aconite, hemlock water-dropwort, opium poppy, black henbane, human fat, and bat's blood.

Notes of Ingress

To fly as a demon, empowered by witches' ointment to assail the non-magical, is a task most easy. Yet, to engage in combat with another witch whilst under such nature of intoxication often leadeth to waking up as a cold, lifeless corpse. In these latter days, finding masters skilled in crafting these salves with precise proportions of each ingredient, with necessary combinations, is rare indeed. When the salve is wrought correctly, one hath but a brief interval before they succumb to the embrace of slumber after its application upon the skin. Hence, the incantations must be brief and swift, designed to convey one's spirit to the destined realm before consciousness doth fade. A renowned incantation of an Italian Lombard witch is thus spoken:

"Unguento, unguento, mandame alla noce di Benevento, supra acqua et supra vento, et supra ad omne maltempo" – "Ointment, ointment, take me to the walnut tree of Benevento, over water and over wind, and over any bad weather."

This is of utmost import, for in the tumult of the mind's chaos, one may lose both direction and control whilst under the salve's potent influence.

In certain traditions, initiatory value is found in witches' salves. A *Hexen* lineage hailing from the Harz region of northwestern Germania giveth ingress into a barbarian-born tradition, by infusing the novice's body with a hot, macabre, vision-inducing energy, a fire thick and black like molten pitch, that the novice must forever cultivate, with receptive meditations accompanied by whispers of repetitious mantic poetry hissed between clenched teeth. Best done in the forest, over heathen burial mounds, or sacred sites found up in the mountains. One season of the Moon passeth; the second stage of the threefold initiation beginneth. *Hexen* instil within the novice a state of dread, before applying the green ointment to the underarms. Thus is the novice cast into a nightmarish landscape to witness the Furious Host of the damned, led by the barbarous spirits Holda and Woden. Forging incorruptible resonance and bond with souls of times long forgotten, an aligning with darker forces.

Anyone may walk this mortal world in spirit, their body left behind. *Hexen* initiation giveth access to another world, a world usually granted access to only those who die in glorious battle. To invite a witch into one's house unblindfolded forever giveth them access to travel there in spirit. Likewise, if a witch visiteth the world of the gods, it is forever within their grasp. Upon waking, the novice is bathed in sacrificial blood of livestock offered to the leaders of the hunt. Having completed the second stage of the initiation, the novice is forever tainted in spiritual darkness and potency, and traverseth this and other worlds in spirit, outside the body, unaided by any salve.

DE PHARMACIS SOMNI ET FLORE NILIACO

Perchance the Greek and Roman sleeping draught of mandrake root steeped with wine was known to some *Mazzeri*. In scant measure, 'tis an aphrodisiac; in excess, it bringeth discomfort, agony, or even death. Yet, in its perfect dose, it leadeth to a deep slumber. And therein lieth the question: doth such slumber bring the wanderings of dreams, or the void of dreamless sleep? A draught or ointment doth play too bold a game of chance for deeds as grave as those of the *Mazzeri*. Yet mandrake's smoke, when breathed, infuseth visions with a subtle grim and macabre hue, a faint touch of nightmare. Beware, for any use of mandrake carrieth risk–its nature fraught with dangers, a hazard to the health of those who dare.

My knowledge springeth from personal explorations, and close acquaintance with those well-versed and practised in witchcraft's arts and lore, who dared to dance with perilous herbs–such as the mandrake.

A more fitting plant intoxication for the arts and combats of the *Mazzeri* might be the blue lotus tea or blue lotus wine, that sacred flower favoured in the Egyptian and Hellenistic mysteries of the goddess *Isis*. Its subtle sway upon the mind, its power to induce visionary

140

dreams, could suit well the ancient dreamscapes in which the *Mazzeri* do their spectral battle.

DE MYSTERIIS ISIDIS ET CULTIBUS COMPARATIS

A faith, born of Egypt, with Rome and Greece did it find new breath, its form near monotheistic in kind. Much like the Christ's creed, it doth centre upon salvation beyond this mortal coil, calling for piety and abstinence. Its followers are drawn to chastity, moral rectitude, and shun the breaking of sacred laws, even as they, when erring, are urged to repent their trespass. A deity reigneth above all, supreme and sovereign; as Yahweh in Christendom doth hold such a throne, so too

Isis in this ancient cult is held divine and high, Mother of Creation and Queen over All. As Solomon's magicians summon demons with Yahweh's many names in holy writ, so too the Egyptians call forth monstrous wights from the Duat, bound to Isis' will, just as with Abraham's god. The art of Christian demon conjuration, *nigromantia*, and exorcism hath its roots in Egypt, not Palestine. Auset, whom the Romans and Greeks name Isis, with Ausar, and most chiefly Sekhmet, Selket, and Bast, be deities who do hold dominion over demons, wielding power to command and summon them forth at will. Albeit, in the conjuring of Egyptian demons, the names of Auset and Ausar may command them, yet such names serve not in works of *maleficia*.

Thus, for deeds of darker intent, 'tis better to employ the names of the dread goddesses Sekhmet, Selket, and Bast, whose power doth more aptly compel and bind such spirits to one's will. The Sphinx-god Tutu standeth preëminent in defence against demons, most chiefly those sent forth by goddesses in magical assaults; Tutu, too, doth wield mastery over demons, holding them well in thrall. Tutu is a god of great avail, an everyman's deity who asketh but for humble bread and, at times, a goose. He wardeth against vile dreams and, by his power, doth shield against ill afterlives, for such realms are but the kin of dreams. Thus was he set by tombs in ancient days, there to keep watch over the dead, guarding their souls in slumber's deep and sacred rest.

The demon-conjurors of Europe in the fifteenth century do practise an art near identical to that of Egypt in the days of the Pharaohs. The European Christian readeth his conjurations from tomes as he summoneth demons, even as the Egyptian read from papyri in ages past. Both do employ strange and potent words, known to no mortal tongue, and issue threats and commands unto spirits, fortified by the power of sacred names of a deity. Magicians of Solomon's craft do wield wooden wands and iron swords to guard themselves from demon-kind; so doth the Egyptian employ wands of hippopotamus ivory and serpents fashioned of copper.

Isis beareth powers akin to Christ: to raise the dead, forgive the errant soul, and offer eternal life to the devout. Her foe, Typhon-Set, tempteth as doth Christendom's Satan, and his form is that of the braying ass, a beast to overcome in faith, much as Christians spurn the Devil. The Egyptians, in their subtle craft, did fashion Yahweh of the Jews and Jesu of Christendom in the likeness of Set, that red-haired and ass-headed god, whose nature was deemed fell and tempestuous. This Set, the dread deity of storm and desolation, whose hand slew his own brother in envy and pursued vile lust upon his brother's son, they did ascribe unto the god of Abraham. From this dread portrayal arose, in the minds of the Gnostics, *Yaldabaōth*, a demon-god of their own imagining. Yet, in their mysteries, the Gnostics did sever Jesu from this grim image, esteeming Him as a being distinct and apart. The Gnostics, a strange and wondrous folk, did fashion a devil-god, akin in nature to *Ahriman* of Persia, yet in the likeness of *Zurvān*, the lion-headed serpent, who reigneth over boundless time and space, and doth transcend both good and evil.

DE ITER MORTIS ET DIVINITATIS AETERNAE

In the sacred temples devoted to Isis, the very air itself seemeth bathed in the hues of gold, blue, and white–such colours as do reflect the purity and majesty of the Divine Mother. Therein lie the mysteries of the Sun, Moon, and the radiant light which doth shine upon the earth, all held in reverence, as too are the waters pure and clear, sanctified by the goddess herself. These colours and symbols bespeak the deeper meanings sought by her devotees, for through them, the divine may be glimpsed, and the path of illumination may be trod.

An initiate may never gain entry unto the mysteries of fair Isis, save if the goddess herself in dream didst first appear. The rite, a solemn passage, demandeth fasting, prayer, the cleansing bath, and abstinence long before the temple's gate were crossed. There, within, the sacred priests performed a ritual over three days, reminiscent of the ancient *Liber Portarum* and *Liber de Transitu Æternitatis*, yet here undertaken by the living, echoing a passage traditionally reserved for the souls of the dead.

Romans observed that this journey bore a striking resemblance to initiation rites in the Mithraic and Greek Eleusinian mystery traditions, which also involved profound encounters with realms beyond the mortal coil, performed with the guidance of priests, who didst bid the initiate behold what lay within the sung hymns, all accompanied by a magnificent display of ceremony. The hymns serve but as the painted tales of visions beheld whilst treading the shadowy paths of the realm of the dead, and betwixt these hymns are interwoven songs wrought wholly of barbarous names. These names, uncouth and strange, are the wayfaring chants and potent charms of the Chaldæan, the Egyptian, the Grecian, the Gnostic, and the mystic of the Hebrews. Iamblichus, that sage most learned, did admonish magicians to render them not into familiar tongue, for their might, he held, was born of their sound and not their sense. At whiles, these names are whispered to be the sacred appellations of whatever god the tradition doth revere, yet no mortal may with surety frame their utterance. It is not the precision of the voice that lendeth power, but the cadence, wrought to entrance the soul, to ensnare the senses, to submerge the spirit deep, and to draw all thought and focus unto the rite alone.

A journey climaxing in an out-of-body experience within the hymn induced otherworldly visions. In the Eleusinian mystery traditions, this rite not only bestowed upon the soul eternal life as a god in the dreams of the hereafter, having successfully traversed the trials of death while yet in life, but also forged a bond with the land itself, by deepening the connection to the ancestral dead who haunt the very soil of the nation. Egyptian and Grecian mystery cults did ever contain a touch of necromantic craft, seeking visions through dreamful trances whilst they lay in slumber within a tomb, 'mongst the relics of the dead, a skull, or by a corpse. The spirit of the deceased did manifest within the visions, to offer counsel and guide the initiate upon their sacred path.

A god of Grecian wisdom did impart unto us that the journey to the underworld, as performed in Eleusinian mysteries, doth find its end in the assuming of a godly form; for through no vision but divine may the divine itself be known. 'Twas by spirit possession that the initiate, enrapt in sacred trance, did see the world as through the very eyes of a god. In manner of Mithraic and Eleusis' mystic rites, so too do the ancient paths of Isis and the Egyptian mysteries confer the splendour of divinity unto the initiate's soul in realms beyond mortal ken. The doors of such sacred initiations stand wide for noble lord and humble thrall alike; yet in life's fleeting stage, the noble remaineth but noble, and the slave no more than slave, even having trod the sacred path. It doth call to mind the crippled beggars, devout Christians, whose every breath and pulse beareth the name of their Christ. To the sanctuaries they journey, day upon day, wringing supplication with fervent tongues. Though their earthly lot be misery and want, they gaze beyond the veil and dream of dwelling in golden palaces in the life to come.

Notes of Ingress

The rites of Eleusis, in their prime, were of equal measure and common standing. In their most flourishing days, as many as three thousand souls could partake in the sacred mysteries at once. Of all estates and conditions, all were welcome—men, women, slaves, and even children. Yet, two conditions held sway over the threshold of entrance. First, each seeker of the mysteries must be versed in the tongue of Greece. Not that they must be of Greek birth, for strangers from distant lands did partake, but they must understand the speech, that they might comprehend the words of the rituals. Secondly, none could enter who bore the stain of unlawful murder upon their soul. No blood, whether of kindred or foe, could mar their hands, for when passing into the land of the dead, or the *Duat*, as the Egyptians name it, the burden of one's unresolved transgressions doth weigh heavy upon the spirit. And this weight, a grievous and unwelcome trial, doth render the soul uneasy and filled with discomfort.

Among the Greeks, 'twas only transgressions of *hybris* that did provoke the wrath of the gods (*goddess Nemesis*). *Hybris*, in their tongue, bore not the meaning of pride as we know it, but rather spoke of acts that humiliate and dishonour another. To lay violent hand upon a person, to steal from a man, or to claim the beauty of a mortal outshineth the divine, was *hybris* most foul. And so, to defile another through rape, to strip them of their dignity, was an affront to the heavens. To mock and insult with vile words or images, rather than seek counsel through reasoned debate, was likewise an act of *hybris*, one that did bring divine judgment upon the offender. For to humble another, especially a god, was to defy the natural order and invite the disapproval of the immortal realm.

Similar otherworldly journeys, akin to the mysteries of Isis, we see in the Jewish *Hekhalot* practices, and the Christian texts *Pistis Sophia* and the *Liber Ieû*, the soul ascendeth the celestial spheres, traversing mysteries usually reserved for the departed. And similar to how the *Benandanti* traverse both the lofty heights and the deepest shadows below, descending to hell's chasms to reclaim souls lost, and bearing them up toward heaven's embrace–nay, through the dreams of the departed they work their art, breathing life anew into those visions and lifting them from the dark. Only the *Benandanti* do so with wondrous ease, lacking the need for aught but their own skill and will, unburdened by the bitter toils and trials borne by the Gnostic, the Hebrew, the Greek, and the sons of Egypt alike.

In this sacred Egyptian sojourn, the seeker doth descend to meet with Isis in the shadow of the underworld, whence she doth guide them to the bright celestial realm, amongst the gods. Thus is the boon of this journey, the promise of salvation granted in the endless life to come. Priest of Isis, Volusius Caesario, doth proclaim that if this alone be done whilst the soul doth part from its earthly coil, then, let the rites or practices by which one cometh unto Isis matter not, for the rite hath surely reached its consummate end. What doth matter most is to meet the goddess Isis whilst in the outer body's state, to beseech Her salvation, and be lifted up to glimpse the realm of the *Ntr*. Thus, salvation is attained and can never be undone.

The goddess is often depicted in sacred likeness, much as the Madonna with her child, wherein the Divine Mother tenderly holdeth her offspring, both a symbol of nurturing grace and boundless love. Such is her visage in ancient art, that she doth embody the essence of creation, the eternal guardian of life, and protector of souls, evoking a sacred bond that echoeth throughout the ages. Thus doth she stand, as Isis with Horus, or the Virgin with Christ, a vision of maternal divinity revered by all who seek her favour.

Theirs is a magic of healing virtue, a power that doth lift curses from the afflicted and peer beyond the veil through divination. Yet, in firm defiance, they stand opposed to witchcraft's art, which they deem a dark and forbidden path.

DE SOMNIORUM POTIONE ET INCUBATIONE SACRA

aily do the devout of Isis kneel before her shrine, offering prayers in reverent devotion. The goddess, gracious and omnipotent, doth answer her worshippers through visions sent by dream. 'Twas common among them to drink of the blue lotus wine (a relaxing aphrodisiac followed by dreamless sleep or vivid dreams), potions with *Syriaca ruta* (no doubt a master alchemist can find the right combinations to avoid the nausea), mandrake mead (poison), and mandrake beer (poison), whose essence stirreth vivid dreams and doth serve as a medium for divine communion. Dream incubation, with rites and potions to enhance such visions, stood central in their sacred practice, for through these dreams, the mysteries of life and death unfolded, and the will of the goddess was revealed to her faithful.

Given the reach of the Roman Empire, it is highly plausible that the cult of Isis could have made its way to Corsica. Oft the dream-world of the *Mazzeri* is journey without the fragile house of flesh, traversing this very world in spirit. At times, the human animal, though unwitting, is granted a fleeting glimpse of second sight, allowing them to perceive our spirit-bodies. Yet, in their folly, they mistake our spectral forms for our mortal physical selves. Thus it is, in many traditions, that we take upon us the shapes of beasts whilst wandering: a flight of butterflies, or a prowling cat. Such transformation is no Herculean feat, for by mere intent and the mind's envisioning, these forms are swiftly assumed, with little effort save the will to shift.

To all I give this eternal gift, this disease without cure that doth the soul afflict. Yet alloweth us to know mysteries unknown on any other road upon this earth. These words alone I give as guidance, to navigate this mysterious path.

PART V

TENEBRAE DRACONIS: DRAGON'S NIGHT

On the Dread Initiation and the Sombre Fire

(Herein is set down the tale of my ingress into a most baleful tradition, veiled in shadows and steeped in sorcery, wherein the ancient Devil Obboney–black serpent and skull-faced sovereign–did mark me as His own, and the purple witch's fire took root within my soul.)

I did follow whispers and rumours of a magical tradition from a far-off land whence my parents once dwelt. At first, I thought it naught but simple laymen's folk-charms and incantations, yet the locals' fear surrounding it urged me to inquire further. From the outside, I perceived no special aspect, nor any uniformity amongst the varied practices of those who claimed mastery. Some worked with no charms, medicines, rites, nor spells, as though the magic were purely of the mind; yet there was a strange purple energy about it, one that unsettled most, though I found myself beginning to crave its very presence.

DE OBBONEY ET ARTE VETUSTA

A certain man, a custodian of that ancient craft, did offer to bestow upon me the power–an initiation, as it were. While many do pay a princely sum for such a gift, he demanded not a single coin from me. He spoke gravely of his witchcraft, declaring it to be an evil power, ever attended by a dark familiar spirit. This spirit, a malevolent deity whom he named Ɔbɔne (*Obboney*), he did describe as the very author of evil, whose influence doth pervade heaven, earth, and sea alike. *Obboney's* power, he said, is "purely for evil and witchcraft," and if displeased by those not initiated in the art, can bring forth cosmic and social calamities upon the world. To appease this ancient black serpent, as he did call it, naught but human sacrifice would suffice.

Obboney, a figure most curious, steeped in gravitas and devoid of jest, doth take pleasure in the terrors and forbidden realities of the supernatural trespassing upon human lives. The entity reigneth over the realms of death and the corporeal plane, yet claimeth not the mantle of a god, preferring instead the shadows where horror and fascination entwine in a dance most eerie.

I did tell the custodian plainly that I had endured witchcraft initiations in times past, and that such rites

154

did come with a grim toll, costing another man his life through unnatural means. In some lineages, such phenomena are known as *Sixpence*. I explained further that though I am content to accept supernatural consequences as the price of initiation, I would not take a man's life by mine own hand for the sake of a tradition of which I had scarce knowledge. He replied, assuring me that no such thing was needful; I need not even offer up the blood of a beast, let alone the life of a man, to gain this witch's power–though all such things can be included, if desired. A number of practitioners do vaunt themselves as godly and devout, their tongues speaking much of piety and righteousness. Yet what drew me most to mine initiator was not the strength of his miracles alone, though they surpassed the common wonders of others, but that he held no desire to cloak himself in the mantle of moral virtue.

I perceived in him a cultivation more untainted and free, unmarred by the trappings of Indian, Muslim, Christian, or Jewish innovations. His art stood plain and unembellished, adhering steadfastly to the witchcraft of its primal roots, as though its simplicity bespoke a truer power.

The custodian did expound that ingress into this craft doth involve the conferring of a malevolent force, one that possesseth the might to bestow all manner of prophetic arts and sorceries. This dark power is summoned and nurtured through the whispered utterance of a chant, and may be wielded with greater potency by channelling an infernal spirit of obscure origin–a spectre reputed by many to be the most reviled and loathsome devil within the lore of a far-off land. A land whose ancient laws condemned such practitioners of malevolence to the cruelest of deaths, not unlike the burning of witches in Europe.

The devil accompanying this power hath a colossal cosmic form that moveth, restricteth, and pervadeth the entire material universe, and a lesser form that is a personal witch's familiar to each practitioner. All practitioners are this devil and must discover their own visage as such. The devil who is *Obboney* delighteth in exploring the diversity of individuals, lands, and cultures.

People are but playthings to amuse the darkness as it manifesteth its magic around them, turning their lives upside down. Some say to speak to this devil one must consume bones of the dead first, or it is better to speak to them in cemeteries. No such custom existeth in the land of its origin. This devil was oft called forth at the base of two very specific species of tree, believed to act as ladders for the dead to climb out of the underworld.

Obboney is oft portrayed as a black serpent or a skull, yet to those newly initiated, it may reveal itself in a single unique monstrous form, varied in its appearance to each individual.

This apparition, dreadful and uncanny, bringeth forth a palpable essence of death and decay, as though the very breath of rotting corpses accompanieth its presence.

Such a vision lingereth near the initiate during the early days of ingress, foreboding and sinister, as a harbinger of the dark and perilous path upon which they now tread.

One cannot shake the lingering sense of unease, a shadowy spectre lurking at the edge of consciousness. The silence and darkness seem to press in around like a suffocating cloak. One can discern they have ventured into the bad lands, whence they feel 'neath the gaze of pure malevolence. Here one must obtain or fashion an image of a serpent, and with intent, offer up the malevolence by placing within a bowl the sanguine heart, liver, flesh, or blood of a beast. This vessel should rest within one's dwelling—most fittingly within one's bedchamber—for the span of a day and a night, wherein the potent energies may gather and take root.

This foul creature, which many an initiate, upon first encounter, instinctively believeth to harbour ill will towards them—nay, to covet their harm or death—is none other than the witch's familiar. It is not *Obboney* the cosmic being, but *Obboney* the familiar spirit: a denizen of that infernal brood to which *Obboney* is akin. Such a spirit may assume any monstrous form or gender, bearing no necessary semblance to the nature or desires of the initiate.

GANGLERI

Though its entrance into their lives be shrouded in ominous dread and menacing energy, it standeth as the witch's ally. For beneath this diabolical nature lieth a bond forged in the fires of the arcane—a steadfast companion whose power, if embraced, may serve the witch well in their craft.

Those who do suffer the torments of madness or drown themselves in the stupor of wine and other foul potations shall lack the clarity of perception to feel the empowerment this tradition bestoweth, and thus be unable to wield it. Likewise, those afflicted by a melancholia born not of circumstance but deeply rooted in their very soul shall most likely be driven to despair and self-destruction amid the agonies of the initiatory ordeal.

For before one may master the energy, it bringeth forth grievous depths of sorrow, demanding from the initiate a cool detachment and fortitude, if they are to survive and endure its onset.

DE PRÆPARATIONE ET TRANSMISSIONE

or twelve nights before the rites of initiation, I was bound to don garments of the deepest black and abstain from all manner of intoxicating draughts and spicy fare. The light of the sun was also to be shunned, despite *Obboney* being a deity of the solar kind. Yet *Obboney's* realm is not the sun that shineth by day, but rather that which journeyeth through the dark underworld–the midnight or black sun, if you will.

Throughout this time, the custodian did perform several transmissions of the witch-power into my body, each bestowed from afar, to prepare me for the impending ordeal.

To infuse my body with the witch's power, that strange and sombre purple energy from afar, the custodian did invoke and channel the dread entity Obboney, all whilst reciting the dark incantation. He did conjure in his mind's eye an image of my form, as though I were present within the very chamber where he did labour. Setting the palms of his hands upon a flat surface, which he did envision to be my body, he did press upon it with intent, as though to push the uncanny energy into mine own flesh and bones, even as he chanted the words of the incantation.

Notes of Ingress

The incantation serveth as a vital means for the witch to invoke and rouse the sombre purple flame that is the witch-power of the lineage.

It doth sustain the alignment with this force and foster its growth. <u>Yet, 'tis futile to impart the initiate with the words of the incantation before the appointed time, for without the initial transmission, the words alone shall summon naught.</u> When first the power is conferred upon the initiate, the custodian may invent and give birth to a new incantation, as they already possess the might to draw from the boundless wellspring of the tradition's mysterious and unearthly sombre witch's fire.

To murmur the words in low whispers, whilst channelling the sombre energy into the initiate's very being, forges a resonance–a key that enableth the initiate to henceforth access the egregoricus stream of enigma that hath been cultivated and deepened through the ages by the lineage. The incantation ought to speak to the essence of the power and be comprised of no more than four brief lines. At times, a custodian shall employ the very chant that was bestowed upon them, which can prove to be most potent. Here is one that I devised shortly after penning these lines:

"Imperium noctis, ex mea voce veni, potens curre per me."

To channel forth the dread purple fire of the witch, one must chant the sacred incantation, intending the current to descend through the arms and issue out from the open palms. The witch's fire is never to be visualised, for to impose a vision upon it would but hinder its natural course. It hath been described as royal purple, for many,

162

when basking in its darksome radiation, do report the energy manifesteth in physical sight as a nonvoluntary hallucination of purple light, especially whilst in dark rooms.

When one groweth assured that the energy doth flow–perchance with a very faint sensation or prickling–then may one proceed to direct it without utterance of the chant.

Should one seek to impart this fire unto another from afar, the likeness of the intended recipient must be visualised, though the fire itself remain unvisualised. The physical palms of the hands are placed upon the imagined body of the recipient, and thus is the power pushed into them, that it may seep into their flesh, bones, and soul.

Throughout this rite of bestowing the witch's power, Obboney did grant my initiator further insight and guidance, for it was not merely an act of empowerment, but also a reading of a visionary nature. Thus, he continued the ritual, four hours at each session, six times in the space of six days, that I might be readied to receive the full initiation.

Before each session began, he would utter these solemn words:

"In nomine Obboneii, te obtestor: fac (initiate's name) veneficam huius lineae in aeternum. Et super quemlibet, sive inter vivos sive inter mortuos sit, qui ausus erit (initiate's name) iter impedire, maledictio generationalis

cadat super stirpem eius, ut posteri eorum, aliquo modo,
fiant hostiae Domino nostro horribili."

Thereafter, he did pour a libation of the blood of
livestock mixed with whiskey or rum and cast three coins,
dodder (*Cuscuta* sp.), and the exotic crown of thorns
(*Euphorbia milii*) into a hole in the ground, as an offering
to Obboney, that the spirit might be propitiated and the
pact sealed with due reverence.

By fate, all who tread upon this path are cast as evil,
for such a way was ever their own to follow. Though they
may forsake its practice in life and abandon its craft, yet
that soul shall remain a villain, not a saint. Yet amongst
villains there be both honourable and base. In this realm,
murderers and thieves find praise, for Obboney careth
naught for the sentiments of men, nor for their notions of
justice or politics. Even the cries of a mother's babe, torn
asunder by dogs through the careless wording of a pact,
stir not the spirit's cold blood. For here, indeed, the
promised favours may come to pass, but how they shall
manifest, the spirit heedeth not human feeling, being as
pitiless as ice.

In the earliest days, before the rite be fully
undertaken, one may often feel the baleful gaze of one's
witch familiar, hovering and floating above, a dark
presence lurking 'bout the dwelling. 'Tis wise at such a
time to make an offering–be it fresh meat or the blood of
poultry or a beast–unto the entity, for such a price must

needs be paid for one's entry into these dread mysteries. This forebodeth the sombre gloom that shall follow, wherein all reality seemeth tainted with a purple hue, a strange pallor which may linger for weeks, nay months thereafter. Macabre visions often appear in those first weeks; beware, for never should one offer up one's own blood to such spirits, lest they take one's own self as naught but sustenance.

SODIRNO

DE RITU INGRESSUS

For the sacred rite of initiation, one shalt procure a staff or cane adorned with the likeness of a serpent, or else carved in its twisted shape.

One shalt attire oneself in garments of the blackest hue and gather the exotic herb anise-star. A drinking horn fashioned from the horn of a bull or goat shall also be needed, along with a fitting source for the life-blood of livestock, that the spirits may be duly enticed and the offerings made aright.

Upon the thirteenth night, with serpent-staff gripped firm in hand, one must stand cloaked in utter darkness whilst the custodian placeth his hands upon one's back, pushing the witch's power into thee. Then the initiate shall invoke thus:

"Obboney, bring forth the familiar and spirits that shall walk with me through the span of mine earthly sojourn."

Then is a libation of anise-star (*Illicium verum*) mixed with a beast's blood poured into a drinking horn, fashioned from the horn of a bull or goat, that the spirits may be entreated to draw near and sup of the offering laid before them.

Thereafter, the initiate must recite the dread incantation nine times over, and then proclaim:

Notes of Ingress

"O Obboney, Ancient Serpent who reigns o'er darkness and realms below, thou skull-faced keeper of bones, who dost unbar and seal the gates, Sovereign beyond the veil commanding spirits–of sky, of earth, and of the depths– take now my flesh and spirit as thine own abiding place, now and unto eternity. Obboney, I summon thee–possess me now, possess me now!"

Thus is the invocation made, beseeching that dread power to take dominion within, binding the soul to the dark majesty and forging a bond unbroken.

Upon these words, the initiate shall enter a state of profound receptivity, envisioning themselves as one with a skull for a visage. It may then follow that the body trembles slightly, or that the teeth do momentarily chatter, as the ancient force draws nigh.

Obboney, being a cosmic force of such strange colossal nature, cannot possess a spirit medium as might the phantoms of the departed or the characters of gods do.

For, being of serpent-kind, Obboney cannot shape human words, but speaketh rather in the mystic language of serpents–a tongue of silent impressions and deep, wordless knowings. When his voice must needs be heard in the form of human speech, it is not he who speaketh directly, but rather the serpent bringeth forth skull-faced emissaries from the realm of the dead, to utter in words the unspoken that must be conveyed.

Notes of Ingress

When one doth seek to converse with and command the witch's familiar, 'tis not in the tongue of mortals that such words are uttered, for it comprehendeth not. Instead, in the serpentine tongue, the speaker must engage whilst possessed by Obboney. Though Obboney doth not articulate in human speech, it possesseth the wisdom to fathom our languages. Thus, Obboney serveth as an intermediary for the witch's familiar, and the one who can summon it forth as the need ariseth.

Whilst one is possessed by Obboney, one may convey and command to a multitude of different spirits with this silent tongue of serpents, including demons of the grimoires and the nature spirits that dwell within the wilds. In this state, the initiated doth wield a power that transcendeth the mundane, allowing them to beckon forth those who haunt the shadowed groves and echoing caverns, forging a bond betwixt realms seen and unseen.

The deeper and more enmeshed one becometh in this state of possession, entwined in unity with Obboney, the greater the power and influence one doth wield over the spirits. In this profound communion, the barriers 'twixt the earthly realm and the ethereal world do dissolve, bestowing upon the initiated a mastery over forces both feared and revered. Thus, in this sacred alliance, one may command the spectral hosts that dwell in shadows and haunt the wilds.

Notes of Ingress

In this rite of initiation, often practised as a vigil but not always so, the witch's familiar, if it hath not yet shown itself, shall make its dark presence known. Another ally spirit may, or may not, appear–perchance a demon drawn from Solomonic grimoires–an entity that may be commanded and bound whilst the Obboney's force courseth through the channeller's soul.

The initiate and the custodian, with whispered breath, shall murmur the dread incantation together, gazing into the darkness and scrying until the first light of dawn. When the sun doth rise, then is the rite of initiation accomplished, and the spirits shall have heard and answered the call.

The rite is ended with the initiate proclaiming:

"In the name of Obboney, I, (initiate's name), tread this path for all eternity, both in this life and the next. And upon any, be they of the living or the dead, who dare attempt to thwart my destiny upon this course, let a generational curse befall their line, that their descendants, in some manner, may become sacrifices unto our dread Lord. Moreover, those who bear no progeny shall find themselves bound as my slaves in whatever realm followeth the demise of this mortal coil."

The initiate is now a custodian and must, for the rest of their life, strive to meditate every day, repeating the incantation until the presence of the gloomy purple energy is felt, and invoking Obboney into themselves. This may or may not cause the teeth to chatter for a few seconds or the body to briefly tremble. The power thriveth and groweth when regularly stirred and used in all manner of sorcery. Spells and conjurations may be wrought whilst channelling Obboney, who doth grant insight and counsel.

When channelling this Devil, merely speaking words becometh spells. Breathing in and blowing cigar smoke unto a charm whilst possessed by the Entity empowereth the charm. Invoking forth and projecting the eerie energy from one's hands or through the gaze of the eyes with intent is another way to perform magic.

A charm may be fashioned, and the gloomy energy pushed from palms into the charm can grant it life. Pacts can be made with Obboney akin to how one can with any Infernal spirit.

Daily cultivation of the power bleedeth into every magical practice, making it stronger. In the early days, or even the first year of initiation, there are those who find themselves in carnal union with a spirit; rare indeed is this occurrence, yet it doth happen. Others, in a fever dream, may grapple and contend with the very spirit of the tradition, locked in a fierce struggle, and find themselves emerging victorious, defeating the spirit–this beareth a potent and traditional symbolism that is not at all blasphemous. Yet not all initiates shall encounter these trials or visions, for each journey doth reveal its mysteries according to its own will and fortune.

The visionary power granted by the intoxicating, sombre purple energy–the witch's power cultivated in this tradition–though immaterial in nature, doth bear some likeness to the flaws of physical substances, such as potions or vision-inducing fungi. While it be a potent tool, it may likewise open the gateway unto paths of illusion and idle fancy. A traveller must exercise discernment and check their wits, lest they wander astray in a labyrinth of phantasms, ever spinning new mythologies without practical end. Every vision must prove it's worth to command our gaze, tempered by the touchstone of what be useful and true in the world of the living.

Though we serve as vessels for the Serpent, the Entity findeth favour in possessing objects or idols, thus anchoring our devotion and strengthening the bond betwixt us. The serpent staff is such an image, often joined by a horn of bull or goat, to hold blood and libations.

Graven images of a serpent may also serve as idols of Obboney, and these may be ensouled by placing them in a vessel brimming with the blood of livestock, there to rest for three nights whilst nightly conjurations are made. By the flame of black candles, one murmureth the incantation nine times, then speaketh thus:

"Obboney, grant unto this vessel thine dread spirit and breathe upon its life; let it see through these eyes and hearken unto what is uttered before it. Here shall it be, where offerings may be brought to thee, O mighty Obboney."

This tradition possesseth a most unique manner of soul-capture. One taketh a bottle and filleth it a quarter full with water, or with wine if one would have the victim wander as though inebriated. Then must one murmur the dread incantation nine times and beseech Obboney to possess oneself. Thereafter, utter the words:

"In the name of Obboney, I do seize the soul of [victim's name] within this vessel, ne'er to be loosed until the glass be broken."

With that, breathe more deeply and fix one's focus upon the bottle, continuing thus until one's eyes perceive the hallucination of a white mist, a vapour drawn into the vessel as if of its own accord–as with all things supernatural or spiritual seen with sight in this tradition– no mere visualisation, but a true vision. Once the mist be seen, swiftly seal the bottle with a cork and place it away in a darkened corner, where it can have no sight of one's dwelling, lest its captive stir and trouble thee.

This same art serveth well for the ensnaring of spirits that do haunt a dwelling. Once the ghost is captured within the bottle, the vessel must be interred beneath the roots of a tree whose kind folklore nameth a gateway to the netherworld. 'Tis said that once buried, it requireth between twenty-four and seventy-eight hours before the spirit's lingering presence doth depart from the abode, its bonds drawn into the earth through the tree's dark passageways. Thus, the restless soul is consigned unto the dreaming of the underworld, and the house is made still once more.

To steal the soul of another shall draw them nearer, making them often visit and speak, as though their spirit be bound to the one holding the bottle. Their steps shall be drawn toward the vessel, as if called by a hidden force. Yet as time doth pass, their strength in the mystic arts shall dwindle, and their health shall falter, the degree of such affliction set by the potency of the spell when the soul was taken. For the art of soul retrieval, the manner is much the same as capture; yet if reclaiming one's own soul, the body serveth as the vessel, and if another's, a bottle is employed, from which they must drink the enchanted draught. The spell, though, must needs be spoken with a mind toward restoration rather than imprisonment, the words chosen to match the purpose of reclaiming what was lost.

In a far-off realm beyond the Mediterranean, southward of Egypt, there stand two ancient trees which Obboney have often utilized as ladders to ascend from the depths of the underworld. One, the Kapok, known in nature's lexicon as *Ceiba pentandra,* and the other, the noble Teak, including species–*Milicia excelsa, Milicia regia,* and *Tectona grandis.* Each of these venerable trees doth emit auspicious energies and blessings, which the seeker may draw into their being by pressing their back against the sturdy trunk and meditating whilst inhaling deeply.

We draw in the essence of sacred trees with the same essential extrasensory awareness and manner as that which we employ to siphon the life-force from the human animal. If one can feel the unseen radiations that a tree, a person, or even a ghost doth emit within one's awareness, then one can draw it in with the breath. Like a vampire drawing forth the life-blood, so too do witches, akin to vampires, nourish themselves upon the life-force of others. Yet, in those early days post-initiation, one's psychic and extrasensory faculties oft remain clouded, dulled by the inundation of a new and intoxicating energy. Thus, these sacred practices are best undertaken only after a sufficient time hath passed–months, or perchance a year–allowing for the full adaptation to the energies of Obboney.

This practice is a meditation, a sacred rite upon the Path of the Serpent. Yet, not all trees are worthy of such communion; certain species bear energies harmful to the unwary. The Teak and Kapok serve as portals to the underworld, akin to the Walnut, Ash, Cedar, and Yew that grace the lands of Europe.

Any tree deemed by a culture as a portal to the underworld–many a rite may be performed in their shadow, with offerings laid for the dead or unto Obboney.

Yet, 'tis the Teak and Kapok, in particular, that allow for the summoning of monstrous entities of Obboney's own kin, to serve as faithful servitors in the commission of malevolent deeds. These spirits, akin in essence to the witch's familiar bestowed during initiation, are summoned and crafted into a vessel or fetish, comprising earth, stone, and branches from the sacred tree, and sanctified and ensouled with the blood of a beast. Such a spirit-dwelling may then be transported to one's abode or gifted to another, empowering the servitor to fulfil designated tasks in that domain.

First, one must set the vessel before the tree, then seat oneself against the trunk, as is customary when meditating with sacred trees in this tradition. The incantation is to be chanted nine times, followed by the invocation of Obboney to enter into one's body. As the meditation deepens, one must focus with steadfast intent to draw forth a new witch's familiar, a process that may require many hours. Success is marked by the vision and sensation of the familiar hovering above. Thereupon, one maketh a libation of blood over the vessel, thus binding the familiar to haunt it, and the vessel may then be taken to one's abode.

Once at home, the familiar is given a task, spoken in the Serpent's Tongue whilst still possessed by Obboney. A second libation is poured upon the vessel, sealing the pact, and the familiar is then bound to fulfil the command. It may further require periodic offerings of food or drink, to be placed before the vessel for the duration of a night, as an upkeep for its continued service.

DE SPIRITIBUS, ARBORIBUS, ET ARTE NIGRA

To summon familiars through meditation with a serpent staff or cane consecrated by pouring the blood of a beast as an offering unto Obboney is a practice not unlike that beneath the sacred shade of Teak or Kapok. Yet, the summoning taketh longer, for the staff serveth as a conduit in place of the tree's ancient power. In such rites, the vessel for the spirit may be fashioned as a small cauldron containing a stone, or as a statue bearing the likeness of a serpent. The ensouling of these vessels followeth the same sacred manner: once the spirit manifesteth, a libation of a beast's blood is poured upon the vessel, thus binding the familiar to its new abode.

A nighttime cemetery stroll amidst the graves is yet another practice of this tradition, wherein the wanderer doth cast three coins upon the ground where the departed lie entombed. This offering to the spirits being made, the wanderer then strolls at a leisurely gait, drifting past the graves, ever immersing deeper in a mindful reverie. Until the spirits of the departed emerge, rising up as apparitions discernible to the eye.

These shades, once made visible, may be addressed in speech, and their ghostly voices may reply, as the living and the dead converse amidst the darkened stillness of the night. 'Tis good to make friends among the dead.

The witches of Obboney are but travellers, roaming many realms far and wide, with no homeland to call the tradition's own. Thus, their sacred sites and holy places are often borrowed from the dominions of other folk. They favour ancient sites, abandoned and forgotten, where long-ago peoples marked these sacred sites in the landscape with stones.

These places are steeped in subtle energies, emanating a strange influence upon the mind, much akin to the effect of potent draughts or drugs, particularly if one lingers there for hours, absorbing the radiations coming up from the earth. In time's passage, some of these hallowed grounds have become so forsaken that heaps of refuse now mar them, yet their emanations still flow unbroken.

These were once the seats of ceremony and initiation, where the forces of the earth swell and ebb in tune with celestial rhythms, and those who wander into their midst, especially during such moments of power, may behold visions conjured from the air, as if the very stones did whisper and unveil the unseen. It is our custom, therefore, to rest upon these sacred grounds, to meditate, pray in the serpent tongue, and even sleep within the circles of stone, seeking that the mysteries they guard be revealed unto us. There, amidst the silent emanations, we await the spirits who govern the place, that they may come forth and commune, opening the secrets of the ages to those who would listen.

Once these sacred grounds and their otherworldly wardens have yielded unto us, we do draw from their hidden founts of power, harnessing the energies therein to fortify our spells and deepen our trances. With the guardians' favour and the place's mystic breath flowing through us, we channel these unseen currents to heighten our craft and step ever closer to the threshold of the spirit world. Thus, do we make the forces of these ancient places our own, entwining our magic with the secret life of the earth and the spirits that dwell within it.

Upon this path, there be neither feasts nor hallowed days marked for our observance. We are unbound by calendar or custom, and may render reverence as we please, to whom we will. Our dread Lord, though possessed of power, proclaimeth not themself a god, but rather a Devil, unadorned by divine pretensions. They do not seek the homage of worshippers, yet their favour and assistance may bring great profit to those who would entreat them. Thus, are we free to walk this crooked course, bowing to no command, save that which our own will inclines.

Another practice of ours is to venture far and deep into the inner realms of the mind's eye, until such time as the awareness of flesh and form doth fade away, so as to free the spirit from its earthly vessel. Thus unshackled, the soul may roam as a phantasmal wanderer to distant lands and hidden places, beholding the world from afar, yet with eyes of the spirit. The cultivation of our lineage's strange purple intoxicating and sombre force, over long years, doth loosen the chains that bind others more tightly, allowing us to move with ease 'twixt realms, where spirits do often tread.

Moreover, such mastery doth render the art of trance and mediumship a ready practice, the possession of spirits an easy habit. Yet, to reap the fullest harvest of our tradition's strange powers, one must give the practice due diligence, surrendering to the trance and inviting spirits to take hold, a few times each week. Thus, may one quicken the development of skill and draw nearer to the boundless gifts that this witchcraft bestows.

Our craft of charm-making doth know few bounds, offering us ample freedom and creative delight. In the shadowed hours of night, I would meet with another witch, and together we would deliberate upon the troubles that beset us. We forged a charm, tailored to address our plight, contemplating its purpose, how it should be nourished and sustained by a simple verbal formula and a daily libation of water.

We did deliberate upon the omens it would impart upon the successful completion of its tasks, as well as the signs it might present to signal its need for further sustenance from our lineage's sombre purple witch fire.

Once we named it, imbued it with character and form, we rendered its likeness in ink upon small parchments to carry as our talismans.

With hands laid upon our individual charms, we engaged in light-hearted discourse for the space of an hour, channelling our lineage's grave purple witch fire through the palms of our right hands into the parchment, thus granting it life as a sentient being. Our creations did always greatly exceed those crafted by the most skilled *Picatrix* astrologers, and even those fashioned by Eastern monks who employed a variety of rare magical materials, including the corpse remnants of the *pactati mortui*.

As is the custom in many paths of witchcraft, we commune with the spirits of our brethren who have passed, not only those newly departed but also those whose mortal coils were cast off centuries ago. These conversations are carried forth through silent discourse of the mind, through dreams wherein phantasms visit, or in the state of spirit possession, wherein the departed take hold and speak through our very lips. Whether these encounters be real or mere fancy, no matter, for it is only the fruits of such communion that bear significance.

The European craft, for reasons not wholly discerned, seemeth most adept at conjuring the shades of ancient souls, as though the passage of time did not sever the bond 'twixt the living and the long dead. Before I embarked upon the study of a Northern Italian tradition, whose mysteries I was initiated into years past, I did summon forth one Paulus Gasparuttus, a notable figure in a lineage, who dwelt once in the Alpine village of Giassico. Of the history I then knew but little, nor did I speak the *lingua Foroiuliensis* of my elders, yet was I aware that this man's name echoed down the halls of history and was well remembered in the records of his time. I did call upon the spirit of Paulus Gasparuttus, and was swept into a waking vision most heavenly, wherein I beheld a castle courtyard, splendid in its glory, that belonged to Paulus in his paradise beyond the mortal veil. There blossomed blue flowers all about, and Forojulian peasants busied themselves, offering loaves of bread at some merry festival. Paulus himself did acknowledge my presence, and though he noted my dealings in certain witchcrafts of which he did not wholly approve, his countenance was kind, and his manner most affable.

In our meeting, he bestowed upon me a blessing and an empowerment, the effects of which have proven most profitable indeed. When he uttered the blessing, he did speak a mighty word, and at once the sky above, laden with white storm clouds, did rend apart, unleashing bolts of lightning and the crash of thunder. His voice did echo forth, powerful as that of a god, as the heavens themselves seemed to tremble at his command. Paolo and I did often converse at length on diverse subjects concerning the *Benandanti*, and much was revealed in our many exchanges. Imagine then my wonderment when, upon reading the Inquisition's manuscripts, I found therein the very same discourse which Paolo had shared with me—his words and dealings with the inquisitors of Rome, all faithfully recorded in that archive. It did astonish me to discover that every matter he had spoken of matched with utmost precision, though before that time I had never laid mine eyes upon those documents nor knew aught of their content. Paolo's wit and merry disposition did shield him from the worst torments the Inquisition might have devised, leaving him free to live out his days in peace. He did depart this world at a ripe age, with riches and strength well kept, his health unbroken even unto his final breath, and a gleam of mirth upon his lips. Yet his spirit doth not appear as an elderly man, but in the full vigour of his youth.

The departed kin of Obboney's craft do speak well of the afterlife, where they seem to dwell in delight, and proclaim that in death, their power hath waxed greater than in their mortal years. Though many souls who perish by their own hand, or by violent means, or suffer grievous illness are wont to wander as tormented spirits, the witches of whom I have knowledge have not been so afflicted. It doth appear that a witch holdeth greater mastery over the fate that doth await beyond the veil, and is not subject to the same helpless plight that befalleth the common soul. In the hereafter, a witch doth shape their own destiny, far freer from the tyranny of those grievous conditions that bind others. Our familiars and gods are still held in close commune by our departed brethren; some do summon their aid often, whilst others leave them idle, yet ever on call should their need arise. One brother telleth me that, though he may have incarnated anew as a man, he doth yet exist as an *antecessor* of our lineage. A sister, meanwhile, shunneth a complete submersion into the heavenly dreaming, preferring instead to keep a watchful eye upon the realm of the living, deeming the blissful heavens to be but a hindrance to the goal of attaining that mystical *Felicitas* of which Henricus Cornelius Agrippa doth speak in his writings upon the occult.

Such discourse with spirits I cannot wholly affirm as genuine, for I do not readily accept the words of the dead until the matters they relate be verified in the material world. Yet I must confess, the counsel they have imparted concerning earthly affairs, both present and to come, hath proved true and reliable thus far. Only when their utterances have been corroborated by evidence in this realm, do I yield to their legitimacy.

DE CUSTODIA ET PERPETUITATE

It is of utmost import to initiate others into this venerable tradition, for through such rites they shall glean the sacred mysteries of our path and behold the vast expanse of its reality. Oft do the fledgeling custodians fret, believing themselves ill-equipped to bestow the gift of the sombre purple witch's power–an essence we whimsically term *witch's fire*, though it burneth not with heat, but serveth as a metaphor for the very energy that floweth through us. As they commence to channel this *witch's fire* into the bodies of their initiates, doubts may assail them, for they scarcely perceive the energy they impart. Yet, lo! In the weeks that follow, the initiate shall experience a profound awakening, as the effects of this sacred rite unveil themselves–an echo of the initiator's own transformation when first they partook. Moreover, they shall observe a remarkable constancy among those they initiate; though each is unaware of the path ahead, their experiences shall converge with little deviation, attesting to the potency of the *witch's fire* and the interconnectedness of our mystical lineage.

What is inscribed within this tome compriseth all that the initiate requireth to grasp the nuances of our sacred practice. Yet it lacketh that potent *witch's power*, which can be imparted solely by a living custodian–the very key to the *spīritūs* of our tradition and the source of empowerment that animateth our rites. To engage in our sacred practices without that macabre, sombre purple energy–an essence steeped in the *memoriæ* of our forebears–is to invoke not the true magic of our lineage.

Much of our craft unfoldeth involuntarily, often accompanied by experiences both surreal and macabre, as side effects of that dread-laden *witch's fire* we so diligently cultivate and draw from. Without this vital essence, one doth not merely practise differently; one findeth oneself adrift, unable to touch the deeper wellsprings of our ancient and profound art. What is inscribed here standeth as the sole compendium of material and instruction upon this path; all else must be divined through intuition as they progress and traverse this winding road. Each initiate shall, in their unfolding, discover the hidden truths that lie within their own hearts, guided by the subtle forces that accompany them on their journey.

PART VI

NOS CONLOQUIMUR CUM MALIGNIS SPIRITIBUS: CONFERENCES WITH SPIRITS

(Here begins the dire account of Zauberer-Jäckl and his unholy kin–a tale of cursed blood, shadowed rites, and the cruel justice wrought by men who feared the whispering dark)

In the dark vale of Werfen, near the city of Salzburg, there lived one Barbara Kollerin, whose trade was the less than flattering work of a knacker–handling rotting carcasses, and unwanted beasts, turning their remnants into goods. Such a calling, base and loathsome to the eyes of the common folk, earned her not the most pleasant reputation. For this foul occupation, the townsfolk held her in bitter contempt, bestowing upon her the scornful title *Schinder-Bärbel*, and her son, by cruel extension, they named *Schinder-Jäckel*.

And like many who walked the path of the poor and the cursed, Schinder-Bärbel held no faith for the Christ, nor fear for His Church. She often robbed its sanctuaries, an offence most grievous, believed by many to assure damnation.

Unbeknown to most, she wielded the arts of a *Hexe*, a witch of malign intent. A nasty beggar, with cruel tongue, she did often threaten those whose wills bent not to her desires, foretelling grievous harm to their kindred should they defy her. And in truth, ill fortune and death did follow in the wake of her curses, striking down the homes of those who stood against her.

In the year sixteen hundred and seventy-five, Schinder-Bärbel, a cunning wench, was caught in brazen thievery, pilfering coins from the consecrated offertory box of a church in Golling. With naught but fish bones and bird glue did she attempt this misdeed, a scheme more crafty than reverent. Her canine companion and young apprentice in crime, fifteen-year-old Paul Kalthenpacher, did serve as watchful sentinels, aiding her daring theft with keen and silent vigilance. Together, this ragtag band held to their clandestine craft, with eyes sharp and souls bent upon the loot within that hallowed place.

They did descend upon poor Bärbel with grievous torments most vile, binding her thumbs in cruel iron screws, and upon her feet they laid twenty kilograms of weight, seeking to wrest from her the truth. In the throes of such agony, Bärbel, though a woman of advanced years, showed naught but fortitude, displaying no tears to the astonishment of the onlookers. Instead, she laughed, as if the pain were but a jest.

Amidst the dark mirth, she confessed to many foul deeds, and, most damning of all, laid bare her own blackened heart, declaring herself a *Hexe*. Aye, she did not stop there, for she named her own flesh and blood, her son Paul Jacob Koller, a *Hexe* as well, skilled in the dark and forbidden arts. Thus did her torturers extract from her lips the admissions they sought, wringing from her words both vile and pitiful beneath the dread weight of their fiendish devices.

Barbara, under the weight of tortures and the threat of swift judgment, confessed to ghastly deeds most fell and foul. She spake of casting dark powders upon the fields, that blighted livestock fell dead under their baleful influence. And as for men and women, she professed to lay tree roots enchanted by black fire upon their land, or worse, to slip from her mortal form and feast upon the spirit of their vital organs, they unknowing and unshielded. She summoned tempests at her bidding to smite the wheat and spoil the crops, and employed charms of theft–even thieving from her kin.

In dark gatherings, she participated in barbarian pagan rites that acknowledged no power in the Abrahamic faith, holding instead to a worldview that deemed those divinities powerless. She named her son, Paul Jacob Koller, a notorious vagabond, a master thief, and a servant of

Lucifer, bound by a most unholy pact. Young Paul Kalthenpacher, her accomplice in crime, corroborated her damning words, as did a multitude of witnesses. Yet it was the thorough investigations that uncovered the truth of her confessed misdeeds, much to the astonishment of those who had initially doubted her claims. Thus, with the weight of evidence upon her, Barbara's fate was sealed. Her sentence: to perish in the flames, and so she was delivered to the cruel fire of Salzburg, where it served as both judge and executioner.

At least, so we are told, Bärbel did confess before the magistrates that her son was a witch. Yet in Austria 'tis known full well that a mother of the craft doth instruct her offspring in the arts of sorcery, beginning when the child is but seven years of age, and at the time of puberty, commenceth their initiation. 'Tis more traditional a daughter be chosen, or an uncomely one, for such a one hath little else to gain favour in this world. Since Jäckel was Bärbel's son, it wouldst have been presumed, without question, that he bore the mark of a witch, for there were no other to inherit his mother's eldritch lore.

The townsfolk are much enamoured of a heretic's flames or the casting of a witch unto the pyre, finding therein a spectacle more wondrous than the playhouse or marionette's show. The more ingenious the cruelty, the larger doth it beckon the throng, swelling in multitude as though drawn by some strange magnet of suffering. Nay, they come with their kindred, babes in arms, to feast their eyes upon the grim spectacle. The nature of the human creature is a curious thing indeed–delighting in pain, in fearsome justice, with a morbid zeal that no earthly revel can outshine.

In the Germanic lands, those who dabbled in divination, healing, and the arts of magic bore not the name of witch, nor did they face the pyre's fiery doom. Fortune tellers and village healers, their craft being deemed of a lesser nature, often endured lighter penalties for their arts, such as fines or other minor chastisements. Yet, the *Hexen*–those who practised the darker arts known as *malefica*–stood apart, for their craft lay in the causing of harm and death by spiritual means. A witch, by the understanding of that age and place, was one who wielded power with malevolent intent, to bring sickness or demise. To lack the capacity to take life was, by the reckoning of that time, to lack the very nature of a true witch. Thus, the title of witch was not bestowed upon those whose magic served merely to heal or foretell, but upon those who, through dark enchantments, dealt in death and ill fate.

DE REGNO UMBRAE

A shadow of death hung over Jacob Koller, for by the name of *Zauberer-Jäckl* was he henceforth known. At the age of twenty, Jäckl was not only bereft of his parents but swiftly found himself among the most sought-after fugitives in the country. His flight to the dense forests and rugged mountains heralded a dark chapter in the region's history, igniting one of the most savage witch hunts ever to scour the Austrian domain. This merciless pursuit spared none, not even the smallest of children, in its ruthless fervour. Though the watchful authorities did chance upon him, wandering in the verdant woods or amidst the throng of the bustling city, he ever eluded their grasp, slipping through their fingers like mist. Each time, they were left to ponder the unsettling notion that he wielded some uncanny power to vanish from sight–either by drawing his sable hood over his head or by casting forth a strange powder into the air, thus cloaking himself in shadow and obscurity.

The authorities' relentless efforts, the resources spent, and the sheer determination with which they pursued Jäckl suggest there was more at stake than a simple case of *maleficium*. Perchance it was naught but the vexation that did plague the authorities, for whenever he was sighted, he appeared as a phantom, eluding capture with an ease that confounded them. Though bounties soared to dizzying heights, the commoners of the streets would not drag him in, standing firm in their devotion, as if he were a cherished wraith, leaving the authorities and Church in utter despair.

The churches throughout Austria and the Alpine lands did earnestly pray that the wicked *Zauberer-Jäckl* might soon meet his end, condemned to burn at the stake for his foul murders and black arts that brought torment upon Salzburg. Yet their pleas, holy waters, relics and bones of the saints, and even prayers uttered by those deemed living saints in Europe availed them not, for no sanctified force could dispel the *malefica* that laid waste to fields, summoned tempests, and loosed plagues of vermin. His dark power caused beasts to miscarry, drew noblewomen into the embrace of beggars, and conjured forth spectral devils, ghastly spirits, and visions of the dead and pagan gods to strike terror into the hearts of good Christian folk. In that age, if aught stirred in the dead of night, 'twas *Zauberer-Jäckl* whom folk did blame, for his name was whispered with dread wherever shadow lay. And some would contend that long after his supposed passing, his presence lingers.

Jäckl earned himself a name as the most infamous witch in all of Austria and the Alpine lands. A man of mystery was he, ever flitting 'twixt shadow and light, seen and unseen, none could say from whence he came or whither he went. His feats of sorcery did stir many a tongue, and his renown spread far and wide, with strange tales told of his marvellous arts and the wonders wrought by his cunning craft.

He rose as a monarch of miscreants, leading beggars and thieves alike under his sway. In the alleys and byways of Salzburg, he did nurture and spread the arts of *maleficium*, his circle of followers drawn from vagabonds, haggard beggars, outcasts, *sodomitae*, and the forsaken souls of Austria's underclass.

The price upon his head did grow ever higher, yet, astonishingly, the poor–though they might betray him for great reward–held their tongues and sheltered him still. It was a war of classes, wherein the chasm 'twixt the impoverished and the privileged grew wider with each passing year. In the latter half of the seventeenth century, Austria herself had just begun to feel the bite of the economic depression that swept across Europe. With resources scarce, and the fruits of labour thin, the ranks of the destitute swelled.

Begging became more than a plea, but a battle of survival. Vagrant youths, filthy and without home or hope, roamed the streets in gangs, pressing upon the fine folk of Salzburg as an ever-present reminder of scarcity's cruel hand. As the cries of hunger grew louder and the desperation more dire, *Zauberer-Jäckl*, once a mere man, became a symbol–a dread lord in the shadowed world of the forsaken.

Jäckl did raise a society of witches among the beggars and vagrants, a wild assembly of the young and the old, hale and ailing alike, drawn to him like moths to the flame of his dark arts. Children and youths made the bulk, yet even the aged lent their ear to his teachings. In the year 1678, it is said that no fewer than a thousand *Hexen* in a city of 17,000 people, aged betwixt ten and fourscore, mostly evaded the authorities; a hundred and thirty-nine, mostly children and teenagers of Jäckl's disciples, met their end burned at the stake in Salzburg.

Jäckl possessed the luck of the Devil, for he was marked with a peculiar favour, rendering him unseen by the eyes of the law. After casting his gaze upon a fair lady whose beauty he could not claim, he encountered Lucifer upon a desolate path. There, the Prince of Darkness appeared arrayed as a knight clad in sable armour, astride a white steed bearing eight legs. From that fell knight did Jäckl receive a charm to conquer the affections of young women of wealth and high birth, far above his humble station.

Thereafter, he beheld Lucifer in manifold guises: once by the gallows, as a one-eyed man clad in black; again at the crossroads, where he appeared as a ragged beggar, barefoot and aged; and beneath the ash tree, he came forth as an ancient barbarian chieftain with Jäckl's face, who communed with a severed head, speaking strange and ominous counsel. Thus did Lucifer's favour find him in every guise, granting dark boons and whispered temptations.

In the summer months, Jäckl's company of witches, masked and with pitchforks, did initiate over a thousand upon the hallowed *Hexenberge*-those sacred witch-mountains that in the days of old barbarian lore were consecrated to the Wild Hunt. Amongst these revered heights was Brocken in the Harz range, known in ancient rites to *Woutan* and *Holda*, and Speiereck, a towering sentinel of Salzburg's wild country. There, beneath moonlit skies, did the dark baptisms take place, purging all Christian waters ever bestowed upon the initiates and casting a spell that made any future baptismal claims of Christ's dominion impotent.

These rites did more than merely cleanse; they imbued the initiates with otherworldly powers, granting them witch-familiars to serve their bidding. Those newly anointed *Hexen* would gain the power to leave behind their physical form and traverse the worlds as beasts of the earth or air, often assuming the shape of wolves or other fearsome creatures. With this power, they joined the host of night, flying forth in spirit, echoing the ancient practices when mortals roamed freely with spirits upon the sacred heights of these *elfriche* haunted lands.

DE IUDICIO ET DAMNATIONE

he Townsfolk, long plagued by fear, didst press mightily upon the authorities, demanding that this villain be found, or at the least, that the ring of sorcery which darkened Salzburg be scattered, for devils and black magic prowled their streets. 'Twas in this desperate hour that Feldner Bettlebub Dionysos, a poor lad of but twelve years, known to all by his cruel moniker, "Dirty Animal," was taken into custody for crimes of another nature. Bent and broken in body, yet cunning of mind, the lad, to ease his plight and gain favour with his captors, did declare that he had knowledge of Jäckl, and, moreover, had spoken with him a mere three weeks hence.

The boy's tale was bold indeed, claiming that not only was Jäckl a sorcerer, in league with the Devil himself, but also the chieftain of a beggars' band, harboured in the slums beyond the city walls. This single accusation, though borne from desperation, was enough to set ablaze the hunt for Jäckl. The authorities, swift to act, did round up all the orphans, the vagrants, and those of ill repute. From Hannerl, a girl of but ten summers, to old Margareth Reinberg, with eighty winters upon her brow, none were spared. All who were taken faced questioning, torture, and most refused to betray the whereabouts of Jäckl.

Their silence, however noble or fearful, was rewarded with naught but suffering: hot irons scorched their flesh, hands were severed from wrists, and screams filled the night. For fifteen long and harrowing years did the terror reign, and in that time, 39 children, from the tender age of ten to fourteen, were consumed by flame, alongside 53 youths, ranging from fifteen to twenty-one years, and over 45 grown men and women. The reckoning claimed 139 souls in all, most of whom were naught but homeless boys, accused of allegiance to Jäckel.

As was the case in other witch hunts of the burning times throughout Europe, the greater number of witches caught were not executed, but rather deported and exiled.

The wretched and forgotten of Salzburg, its orphans, its homeless, and its forsaken youth, didst meet their end in fire and blood, hanged, beheaded, or torn asunder, as the executioner's cruel art demanded. 'Twas a costly affair indeed to see the penniless destroyed, for the debts of their incarceration, trials, of peat and wood for their pyres, and of the executioner's fee, all fell upon the townsfolk, who murmured often on the expense of killing those with naught.

Veni

Notes of Ingress

Few things lie beyond the reach of an oppressed and desperate underclass, whose philosophy is stark and resolute:

"Nos nihil sumus, et ex nihilo venimus. Nihil nos impedit, neque quidquam est quod non audeamus aut perficiamus. Ex nihilo formati sumus, et in illo nihil viget nostra virtus, nulla lege aut metu obstricta."

For when men and women are driven to the brink, with no station or dignity left to lose, what force can stay their hand or quell their spirit? They know no bounds, for there is no deed too dire nor course too grim that they will not pursue, being unshackled by fear and unbowed by fate.

The Zaubererjackl Trials, most grim, plunged the land into a tempest of accusation and terror, a span of fifteen long years marked by the Inquisition's dire hand. From the year of 1675, until 1690, did the region witness with trembling hearts the fates of 139 souls, condemned to fire, to gallows, to the cold grip of death—youth and elder alike—no heart spared by the fervour that swept through Salzburg.

At length, the Inquisition began to grow weary, for the unending tide of black sorcery that plagued Salzburg had taxed even their most zealous efforts. Thus, their fervour waned, and the dreadful march of executions slowed, as exhaustion took hold and the fires of justice dimmed before the darkness they sought to quell.

By the year 1730, the persecutions for witchcraft in Austria had all but ceased, and the fires of the pyre grew cold. The last notable trial of its kind, that of one Maria Pauer, took place in 1750 within the borders of Salzburg, a domain then lying beyond the Austrian realm.

Maria Pauer, a humble maid of Mühldorf, dwelling in the St. Catherine suburb, fell beneath the shadow of accusation in the year 1749. Her misfortune began with a simple errand undertaken at her mistress's behest, yet upon her return, the household to which she had journeyed was beset by uncanny disturbances, whereby strange and dreadful poltergeists did trouble the peace. Suspicion fell swiftly upon the maiden, and soon thereafter she was taken into custody, accused of wielding dark arts.

Within the cold confines of her imprisonment, the harshness of the place did soon afflict her spirit, rendering her weak and forlorn. For two long months, her interrogators, relentless in their pursuit, assailed her with 527 questions, and under the cruel persuasion of torture, she at last confessed her guilt. In the September of 1750, her fate was sealed, and upon the sixth day of October, she was brought to her end, meeting the headsman's blade before her body was consumed in the purging flames.

Her trial, amidst a time when witchcraft's spectre yet haunted the region, saw likewise the fate of Anna Maria Zötlin and Liesel Gusterer, who too were condemned and executed the year prior. Pauer's tragic end marked one of the final echoes of the great witch hunts in those lands, as soon after, such trials did dwindle and the fires were extinguished by the law's decree.

Zauberer-Jäckl himself was last beheld as an aged old man in the streets of Salzburg in 1754, still tangible and mortal, and not some spectral wraith. Thereafter, Empress Maria Theresa's decree of 1768 abolished witch-burning and torture, bringing an end to the age of the witch hunts.

Jäckel, that notorious sorcerer, whose name was whispered in fear and wonder, grew renowned for his unholy arts, by which infernal powers he could conjure at will. 'Twas said that Lucifer himself did possess him as he pleased, for Jäckel called the foul spirit at his beckoning. Through these dark miracles, he eluded the grasp of all authority, growing to a grey old man untouched by the gallows or the stake, strong and healthy, living out his days in freedom, though his name became a curse upon the lips of men.

Hark! There lies no grave for Jäckel, for still do Austrians ponder, in this very day, whether he does breathe or hath departed this mortal coil. Had there been a tomb, the restless spirit of Jäckel would be vexed eternally, disturbed by the conjurings of common magicians. These folk magicians, in their art of necromancy, often invoke the prayers of Christ, though such rites avail naught if the spirit they seek to raise be one of heretical or pagan bent, or a soul that hath rejected faith. Nay, though one does seek to stir the dead by rousing their wrath through the twisted recitation of the Lord's Prayer, uttered in reverse, it is but a senseless folly. For such incantations, where belief is wanting, are naught but empty breath, and their power doth crumble to dust. Whether Jäckel still walks amongst the living, or whether death hath claimed him, he hath found a certain immortality, for in the minds of the people, his name and his legend endure, untouched by time.

Whether Jäckel yet draw breath or lie entombed in death's embrace, his spirit doth haunt these very pages, and in some manner, the realms of those who've perused the words inscribed upon them. For Jäckl's life is endless, and death's cold grasp can never claim him.

Be Jäckel alive or dead, he is here now! The nature of the spiritual realm being what it is.

In the days of Jäckel, the witches of Salzburg received voiceless familiars of the mountains known as *Gangerl*, spirits unconfined by place yet ever met at sacred heights. Through rites of initiation, which cleansed away the waters of Christian baptism, these spirits entered into the witch's company, ever following in unseen step wheresoever the witch might go.

In later Christian fables, such spirits were softened into the image of friendly gnomes, but in older lore and the secret art of witches, they are dark and strange beings–pitch-black in hue and standing no more than three feet tall. Among the Alpine folk, the Devil himself is called *Gangerle*, a name that springs from *Gangleri*, the wandering guise of *Woutan*. This connection lendeth the spirits a kinship with the wayfaring god of Old.

Known for their wayward tricks, these familiars raised clamour in households, tossing pots and pans into disarray and filling the air with violent rushes of wind and rustling sounds. Miners, toiling in the deep earth, oft spoke of meeting these beings, who played upon the senses with such cunning that shadows seemed flesh, and spirit wore the guise of mortal form.

Land spirits play a significant role in the spirituality of various European peoples. These creatures are always dangerous, capable of bringing death; and seldom are they deemed gentle, save in the fanciful tales spun for children, and even there, their nature often retaineth a shadowed edge. There is little point in speaking at length about these spirits, for their essence cleaveth unto the soil that bore them, each tied to place as roots to earth. Yet some, like the *Gangerl, Drude,* or *Alp,* may traverse the seas in thrall to a witch, bearing their malice beyond their native bounds.

When a wayfarer doth set forth upon uncharted lands, he holdeth the greater advantage, as did the Norse who first graced Iceland's rugged shores, or the Saxons who claimed the lands of England, or the Lombards who did make Italy their home, and the Visigoths who cast their lot upon Spain's sunlit plains. It is by forsaking the mortal coil, that the spirit doth journey forth, unseen, to roam the land in ethereal form, beholding the spirits that haunt the hills and dales. In spirit's guise, he approacheth these spectral beings, to learn their true nature, before he doth decide whether his dealings with them are meet.

PART VII

LUCIFER

On the Origins and Occult Unveiling of Lucifer

Lucifer, an odd and curious name, beareth in its root a tale most strange. In ancient Rome, 'twas no more than the name given to the morning star–a male face to fair Venus, that bright and innocent celestial flame, whose gentle light guided sailors upon the sea and stirred the hearts of poets to sing its praises. A deity benign, of little weight or consequence, in those pagan times.

Yet as the Church of Christ made its way to the southern lands of Europa, those learned founders of the faith, labouring over the sacred texts, sought to render Hebrew scripture into Latin's tongue. It was then that Origen Adamantius, a pious scholar and founder, who in his zeal had made himself a eunuch (Founding Christian Fathers shared some views with the Cult of Atargatis), took quill to parchment and, in translating the Book of Isaiah, spake of a fallen king of Babylon. In that text, the prophet named the king *the morning star*, and in Latin, that star is called *Lucifer*.

Thus, the innocent name of a minor male Venus deity became bound with darker meaning, for this passage, meant to mark the fall of a mere earthly monarch, was now yoked to the very Devil in the mind of Christendom. Yet curious is the error, for in the Book of *Revelation*, 'tis none other than Jesus of Nazareth who calleth Himself the Morning Star. By Origen's hand, and through such a twist of translation, the Emperor of Hell became known to Europe by the name *Lucifer*, and thus was the light-bringer entwined with the lord of darkness.

Among the Luciferians, as well as certain other Gnostic sects, *Lucifer* is beheld as a bringer of light, a divine figure who stood in defiance of a malevolent *demiurgus*, the monstrous creator of the material realm. *Gnosticism* presenteth an interesting paradox, for the name itself denoteth not the branch of Christianity that prevailed to become the orthodoxy, but rather those who found themselves outside the fold. In truth, no form of Christianity resteth upon *Gnosis* in its purest sense. It is rather the meditations and contemplations of Plotinus that might rightly be called belonging to *Gnosis*. Yet those practices ascribed to the so-called Gnostics bear not the mark of any true *Gnosis*.

No doubt, the name *Gnostic* shall, by less discerning minds, be most tragically misapplied, leading them to mistake Plotinus's lofty *deictic* method for the creeds of those so-called Gnostics. Alas, 'tis a grievous error, for his contemplations aimed at divine unity with the *One*, and bore no kinship to the tangled mythologies of the Sethians. Even the much-vaunted *Evangelium Thomæ*, for all its praise, is a work most lamentable and lacking in true illumination, held aloft merely by the faults found in the orthodox gospels, whose riddled imperfections make any alternative seem more profound by comparison. Thus, the Thomas text is but a shadow given substance by the deeper darkness of others, rather than a light in its own right. There be but so many defences one may contrive for the sayings in the hundred and fourteenth of *Evangelium Thomæ*, yet none hold substance nor carry weight. Each argument fadeth like mist at dawn, leaving naught but the hollow words themselves to crumble under their own folly.

At the zenith of *Gnostic* endeavour, whereunto the *Libri Ieû* and *Pistis Sophia* do guide the seeker's ascent, is the chanting of hymns–no fair melodies, but rather a torrent of barbarous and unseemly names, devoid of meaning to mortal tongues. By this cacophony of syllables is a vision conjured, revealing a realm beyond the veil, wherein the soul, unshackled with wayfaring art from its carnal shell, doth journey as a spirit-born traveller.

Like the ancient *Libri Mortuorum Ægyptiorum*, the aspirant must pass through many gates in this otherworldly sphere, eluding its monstrous guardians by wielding seals and invoking names long committed to heart. At the last and final gate, the soul doth confront the profound mystery of the *Evangelium Judæ*, which proclaimeth that the pinnacle of attainment cannot be wholly grasped until the body succumbeth to physical death.

Thus, the *Gnostic* doth climb these unseen realms, cleaving yet to Christian virtues in their earthly walk, that, in death, they may at last unite with the god they hold as the one true essence divine.

These be the arcane mysteries of the Gnostic schools, unveiled to none but the initiated; all else is but the diverse philosophies of communion with their esteemed one true god, the speculations of celestial order, and the precepts of earthly virtue.

The transcendental practices of divine tranquillity and stillness of mind, that self-emptying which doth make one a vessel of god, as found in the mysticism of Catholic Saints, the *Hesychastæ*, or in the striving for perpetual felicity—the noble aim of Christian Occultists such as Agrippa—these are things that cannot be achieved through intellectual contemplation, nor by the pondering of philosophy, nor by the art of wandering in celestial realms. Such things are not to be found in any *Evangelium Gnosticorum* or text, nor are they taught in the mystery schools of the Gnostics.

This work here, however, belongeth not to the tenets of Gnosticism, for Gnosticism doth stand in opposition to the arts of divination, astrology, and witchcraft, scorning such practices as the shadows of deception. Herein, the *Lucifer* that manifesteth is one entwined with *maleficium*, a spirit of darker arts, that traverseth both the sacred and profane, a guide through the mysteries that span beyond the bounds of Gnostic thought, though that is no great feat.

The mystical and *gnosis* of this *Lucifer* shall not be revealed here, for it is not the season to lay bare such secrets. Instead, we shall but touch upon the threshold of his being–an entity formed of black fire and majesty, whose ingress doth kindle the soul's deepest yearnings. This spirit of flame and darkness, whom some do call light-bringer, doth embody a power both terrible and divine, yet the knowledge of his mysteries remaineth beyond this telling, veiled from those not yet prepared to receive it.

At the darkened masked assemblies of the *Hexen* upon the *Speiereck*, there doth a strange ritual unfolds. There, a witch is seized by the spirit of *Lucifer* himself, who holdeth sway over the mountain spirits, known to haunt that place. These spectres are called "*Gangerl*"–pitch-black, stunted figures no taller than two or three feet, resembling little more than shadowy men. Much like the mermaids conjured by heathens to be glimpsed amidst the foaming waves upon distant shores, these spirits can deceive the senses into perceiving them as flesh and blood.

Notes of Ingress

As the initiation commenceth, the neophyte is brought forward, flanked by two stout men armed with pitchforks, as if to guard against unseen perils. Thus, the rites proceed, binding the uninitiated closer to the eldritch and infernal secrets of the mountain. The place whereon the neophyte doth stand is naught but an open portal, a doorway through which spirits may pass, and hath been employed in rites of olden times. In the guise of a *Hexe*, *Lucifer* himself doth pour sacrificial blood upon the unknowing soul, bidding them, "See with both eyes open." The men bearing pitchforks then depart, and the circle of *Hexen* doth encircle the neophyte, spinning them around until a possession taketh hold.

This possession may reveal itself through a dark and wicked laughter issuing from the neophyte's throat, and at times, *Lucifer's* voice may be heard speaking a few words through them. The neophyte, unawares until this very moment, knew not that this ritual would plunge them into the grip of such an infernal spirit. Thus, the rite unfoldeth, drawing them deeper into the mysteries of the damned.

LUCIFER

A *Hexe*, possessed by *Lucifer* himself, doth wield a stone of the hallowed ground, marking upon the neophyte's back a slight wound, thus naming them anew– a name born of lineage, reflecting the beastly form wherein the spirit of the neophyte taketh flight. This dark baptism bringeth forth a *gangerl*, a familiar bound to serve, and washeth away the waters of Christendom, undoing any Christian baptism. Yea, not only for the neophyte, but the very bindings of faith shall loosen for their kindred most near, as a later consequence of the rite.

For such revelations ensue, as to unravel the Christian mind's simple creed, revealing the world in new and dreadful clarity. The neophyte's eyes, now opened to see what once lay hidden, gaze upon truths that cannot be dismissed nor ever forgotten

Amen

BIBLIOGRAPHY

Books:

1. Broedel, Hans Peter. The Malleus Maleficarum and the Construction of Witchcraft: Theology and Popular Belief. Manchester: Manchester University Press, 2003.

2. Carrington, Dorothy. *The Dream-Hunters of Corsica*. London: Weidenfeld & Nicolson Ltd, 1995.

3. Dengg, Michael. *Lungau Folk Life: Descriptions and Folk Customs, Stories and Legends from the Lungau*. Tamsweg, 1913; revised by Josef Brettenthaler, Salzburg, 1957.

4. Ginzburg, Carlo. *I benandanti: Ricerche sulla stregoneria e sui culti agrari tra Cinquecento e Seicento*. Torino: Einaudi, 1966.

5. Gri, Gian Paolo. *Altri modi: Etnografia dell'agire simbolico nei processi friulani dell'Inquisizione*. Trieste: EUT, 2001.

6. Nardon, Franco. *Benandanti e inquisitori nel Friuli del '600*. Trieste: Edizioni dell'Università di Trieste, 1999.

7. Vernaleken, Theodor. *Mythen und Bräuche des Volkes in Österreich*. Wien, 1859.

8. Häll, Mikael. (2013). Skogsrået, näcken och djävulen: Erotiska naturväsen och demonisk sexualitet i 1600- och 1700-talens Sverige. Stockholm: Malört förlag.

Websites:

1. ADECEC. "Le Mazzerisme et le folklore magique de la Corse." Accessed June 19, 2025. https://adecec.net/parutions/le-mazzerisme-et-le-folklore-magique-de-la-corse.html

2. Latin Library. "Origo Gentis Langobardorum." Accessed June 19, 2025. https://www.thelatinlibrary.com/origo.html

3. University of Chicago Journals. "Article." Journal of the History of Ideas. Accessed June 19, 2025. https://www.journals.uchicago.edu/doi/10.1086/720176

www.ingramcontent.com/pod-product-compliance
Lightning Source LLC
Chambersburg PA
CBRC100735150426
42811CB00065B/1894